Rugby Football

on old and modern picture postcards (and a selection of other collectables)

Published by Reflections of a Bygone Age, Keyworth, Nottingham, May 2023

Printed by Adlard Print & Reprographics, Ruddington, Nottinghamshire

All rights reserved. No part of this book may be reproduced or transmitted in any form or by any means without permission in writing from the publisher.

A selection of playing cards in Rugby ball shape can be found in the book. I came across these at an antiques fair somewhere, but haven't yet cracked the rules of playing the game!

An incredible journey through 120 years of Rugby images

1. A French cartoon from the 1920s. The players look exhausted and dejected - even the ball appears finished! The artist signed 'Boby' - see page 53 for another cartoon in the same series.

Front cover pics:
(top): In 1912 the Springbok (South African Rugby Union) team toured the British Isles for the second time. Newport beat them 9-3 in front of a crowd of 18,300 at Rodney Parade on 24th October. Fred Birt scored all the points with a try, conversion and drop goal. It was one of only three matches the Springboks lost on that 27-match tour. A local publisher quickly put out a postcard of the local heroes, and on 30th October this example was posted from Caerleon to a Mr Harrison in Gateshead. *"I am sending you this P.C. thinking you might like it. You must be sure and see the S. Africans when they are in Ncstle* (Newcastle). *I have seen 3 of their matches and think they are a fine team. All of them are very fast"*. He then added about the team photo: *"The forward immediately behind Martin (with the ball) is Dibble, last year's English captain"*.
(bottom): Donald McGill was a famous and prolific postcard cartoonist, who designed for the medium between 1905 and 1962, the year of his death. He was dubbed 'The King of the Seaside Postcard' but had a much wider repertoire than that, including a number of rugby-themed designs. His enthusiasm for the sport remained undiminished despite his having to undergo a foot amputation after a rugby injury sustained while playing for Blackheath Preparatory School.
(left): Jack Harrison of Hull FC. **(right):** William 'Dusty' Hare of Newark, Nottingham, Leicester and England.

Back cover pics:
(top left): comic postcards of rugby players frequently depicted them as menacing and huge. This design, by un-named artist, imagines a beefy fullback about to tackle a diminutive centre.
(top centre): Rugby came back into the Olympics, at least in seven-a-side format, in 2016, but prior to that its previous inclusion was in 1924. This art postcard by French artist Rouwy was part of a set featuring various events in the Paris Games that year.
(top right): Stuart Barnes lifts the Pilkington Cup after his team Bath beat Leicester in the 1989 RU Cup Final. Card published by Enterprise Postcards.
(bottom left): this card was published by Raphael Tuck, the pre-eminent postcard producers of Edwardian Britain, in 'Oilette' series 1746, a mix of Association Football and Rugby designs. This scene, painted by S.T. Dadd, shows a dramatic moment in a game. This design is not difficult to find, even today, but the card illustrated is unique. It was sent by W. Reginald Bray, an eccentric collector who earned himself the soubriquet 'The Autograph King' because of his penchant for mailing postcards to celebrities and asking them to return the card to him - presumably in an envelope as there is only one postmark on the card. Bray posted this one on 13th October 1906 to Henry Daneel (a forward who played for Western Province) at Richmond Athletic Ground. Daneel duly signed and returned it.
(bottom centre): Rupert Besley produced this design for a Welsh audience, but it was later provided with English and Scottish references for sale in those countries.
(bottom right): J.M. Staniforth was a cartoonist for the *Western Mail*, and in the Golden Age of picture postcards, his work adorned these magic miniatures. One famous series he illustrated featured caricatures of leading Welsh rugby clubs, cards which are extremely rare today. The one illustrated shows an Aberavon player and has a caption in what was known as 'write-away' style, where a few words were provided which both acted as a caption and a spur to the writer to add something. In this case it was *'I seize this opportunity'*. The postcard was posted at Newport in July 1904 by Lil, a girl who was apparently at a convent boarding school, to her brothers in Roath, Cardiff. She told them how much she was missing them and then added: *"The nuns are very kind. They gave me a cup of tea yesterday. It was horrid stuff. It was too weak, had too much milk & to crown it all it had sugar in it. I wanted to put it outside the window but couldn't"*. On the front of the card she asks the boys *"Do you place yourselves in such a graceful attitude when you play football?"*

2. Rugby lent itself to after-match images of players worse for wear, sporting full-on injuries. This one is by Scottish artist Martin Anderson, who styled himself 'Cynicus', in keeping with his left-leaning outlook on politics and the upper class. This design was overprinted with different place names to give it more local appeal, in this case Troedyrhiw near Merthyr Tydfil.

Union and League - in harmony at last?

29th April 1995, Wembley Stadium, London. Wigan win their eighth consecutive Rugby League Challenge Cup Final, beating Leeds 30-10 in a reprise of the previous year's Final. Wigan's all-conquering team of the late 1980s and early 1990s was captained on that day by scrum-half Shaun Edwards. Coming off the bench after nine minutes was 19-year-old loose forward Andy Farrell, already three years into his stellar career with the club. Two of Wigan's tries that day were scored by Jason Robinson on the wing.

11th February 2023, Aviva Stadium, Dublin. France are playing Ireland in the second of that year's Six Nations internationals. The countries are rated 2nd and 1st best in the world. Before the match broadcast, Shaun Edwards, the defence coach for France, and Andy Farrell, head coach for Ireland, appear on television to talk about their respective teams' prospects. Ireland win the match 32-19. They go on to win the Grand Slam.

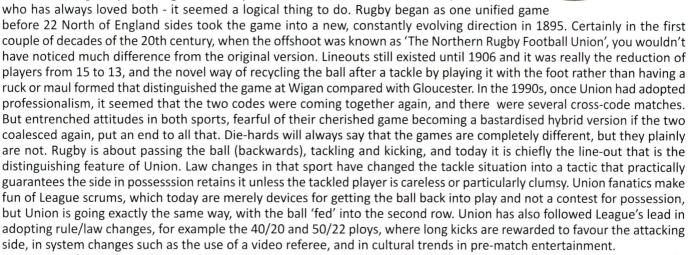

Nothing could better illustrate the coming together of the two codes of Rugby than the scenarios above. I have no doubt that I will have alienated die-hard supporters of both Union and League by choosing to include postcards of both codes in this book, but to me - who has always loved both - it seemed a logical thing to do. Rugby began as one unified game before 22 North of England sides took the game into a new, constantly evolving direction in 1895. Certainly in the first couple of decades of the 20th century, when the offshoot was known as 'The Northern Rugby Football Union', you wouldn't have noticed much difference from the original version. Lineouts still existed until 1906 and it was really the reduction of players from 15 to 13, and the novel way of recycling the ball after a tackle by playing it with the foot rather than having a ruck or maul formed that distinguished the game at Wigan compared with Gloucester. In the 1990s, once Union had adopted professionalism, it seemed that the two codes were coming together again, and there were several cross-code matches. But entrenched attitudes in both sports, fearful of their cherished game becoming a bastardised hybrid version if the two coalesced again, put an end to all that. Die-hards will always say that the games are completely different, but they plainly are not. Rugby is about passing the ball (backwards), tackling and kicking, and today it is chiefly the line-out that is the distinguishing feature of Union. Law changes in that sport have changed the tackle situation into a tactic that practically guarantees the side in possesssion retains it unless the tackled player is careless or particularly clumsy. Union fanatics make fun of League scrums, which today are merely devices for getting the ball back into play and not a contest for possession, but Union is going exactly the same way, with the ball 'fed' into the second row. Union has also followed League's lead in adopting rule/law changes, for example the 40/20 and 50/22 ploys, where long kicks are rewarded to favour the attacking side, in system changes such as the use of a video referee, and in cultural trends in pre-match entertainment.

But if the administrators of both codes tried to ignore and even persecute the other (for a century, Rugby Union banned people who'd even had a trial for a League team from any involvement with Union as player, coach or even spectator), the players have always been eager to cross the code divide. Until 1995, when Union in Britain went openly professional, it was one-way traffic from Union players - principally in Wales - who wanted to secure financial stability for their families by being paid to play a sport they excelled at. There was a long tradition of that exodus north which accelerated from the 1960s, with lots of Rugby Union internationals, including Jonathan Davies, Alan Tait, David Watkins and John Bentley changing codes. After 1995 the trend was for League stars to try their hand at Union. Examples included Henry Paul and Martin Gleeson, but arguably the most high-profile was Jason Robinson, who'd played in that 1995 Challenge Cup Final, whose RU career highlight was scoring the only try of England's World Cup-winning match in 2003. Recently, ex-Wigan RL player Chris Ashton highlighted the success of his move to Union by becoming the first player to register 100 tries (playing for four different clubs) in the RU Premiership when he scored the second try of a hat-trick for Leicester against Exeter in May 2023.

It is, though, the ever-growing influence of ex-League players in Rugby Union international level coaching that has been the most striking trend over the past 20 years.

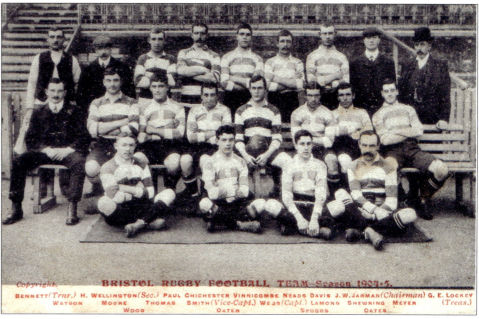

3. Bristol Rugby team from season 1904-5, with the players' names helpfully listed (this wasn't always the case). The postcard was published by Art Printers Ltd of Bristol.

My own introduction to rugby came on a sunny August evening at Lawkholme Lane, home of Keighley Rugby League Club. I'd heard that the school I was about to go to played a game I'd never previously heard of and felt I ought to see what it was all about. At the time I didn't realise that Keighley Grammar actually played Rugby Union, on the other side of the then apartheid divide with Rugby League. I believe I went to the match by myself (I can't remember my Dad taking me and none of my friends in the village of Steeton had heard of Rugby either) and I was instantly captivated by the magic laid out in front of me. Crunching tackles, end-to-end running and passing, a thrilling atmosphere and a clutch of heroes to adopt. Batley were the visitors, but it was the home side that I instantly latched onto, including Terry Hollindrake, who I later discovered was the only Keighley-born player ever to represent Great Britain!

So I played Rugby (Union) at secondary school, then for Skipton (RU) and later centre, full-back or stand-off (sorry, fly-half) for club teams in Nottingham. I'd have liked to have played RL as well, but somehow it just never happened. I ran rugby teams at the schools where I taught, but my best moment came in setting up in 1976 a brand new rugby club (RU) in the Nottinghamshire village where I'd settled, Keyworth. Within a decade we were running five teams and had encouraged hundreds of people to play the game. We roped in school leavers, teachers, miners, accountants and builders. Unfettered by the old boys' hang-up, the club was truly demographically democratic. In 1993 a junior section was started, which is still thriving. Three other clubs were initiated by players who left Keyworth to do pioneering work in their own villages.

The last few years have been incredibly fast-moving ones for both codes of Rugby, which had split irrevocably in 1895 after a massive family quarrel at a pub, albeit with half the family missing! The location was the George Hotel, Huddersfield, and the family was called the Rugby Football Union. The invitations had only been sent, though, to a few members, and all of them were based in the dark satanic North of England, where coal mines and textile factories controlled the purse-strings, and owners with profits to make and shareholders to satisfy called the shots. These few clubs wanted to compensate players for time lost at work when matches were on, but the RFU governing body was having

4. An artistic French postcard by 'P.B.', featuring action from a match, posted from Paris to Bordeaux in 1906.

none of it. The game was amateur and that was that. So a group of 22 clubs formed the Northern Rugby Football Union and began to carve out their own, more free-flowing and spectator-friendly game on their own terms. In 1922 it was renamed the Rugby Football League, and this upstart version dominated the North of England for decades while the two codes remained implacably hostile. Despite this, there was a regular flow of Union players, especially from South Wales, to the Northern Union clubs, lured by the chance to earn a living playing Rugby, from the start of the 20th century. The RFU banned anyone who had ever played League, even at amateur level, from its own clubs' premises. By the mid-1990s, though, the RFU had to examine its own navel. It had been obvious for years that Union players had been remunerated for playing the game, via 'boot money' (allegedly a widespread practice in Wales) or being found well-paid jobs. The game went professional in New Zealand and South Africa in the early 1990s, and the RFU had to reluctantly follow suit to keep its players and raise standards of fitness and skills in competition with countries whose practitioners had become full-time athletes. Rugby Union's conversion to professionalism inevitably brought down the barriers with League, and relations between the codes improved to the extent that cross-code exhibition matches became quite popular. The two games between Wigan and Bath in 1998 were the most high-profile of these, played at Maine Road, Manchester and Twickenham using each code's laws in one of what were most definitely games of two halves. For a while there was talk of merging the codes under hybrid rules, but that idea seems to have disappeared for the present.

In the 1990s, Rugby League also underwent a seismic change, inaugurating a concept called 'Super League' in a controversial deal with Sky TV, which had offered what seemed at the time a colossal sum of money to an impoverished sport to screen the games. The aim of Maurice Lindsay, who negotiated the deal on behalf of the RFL, was to re-organise some of the traditional clubs into regional groups, but this met with fierce resistance and was shelved. Fans of Wakefield, Featherstone and Castleford went ballistic on hearing they were to become 'Calder' and there was similar opposition from traditional clubs like Warrington, Widnes, Workington and Whitehaven. Another of Lindsay's visions, the introduction to the top flight of Rugby League of teams in London and Paris, did happen, though, because it was integral to the 'Super League' concept. Sky TV still effectively bankroll the RFL and call the shots.

5. Another French postcard with a Rugby image, with appended advertisement.

Change was also happening at Lawkholme Lane. In 1991 my hometown club was re-invented as Keighley Cougars, with two local businessmen determined to raise the club's fortunes, which had dipped to near-invisibility in the late 1980s. Mick O'Neill and Mike Smith renamed the ground Cougar Park and introduced pre-match entertainment in the style of American Football games. Once Super League began, this became the norm at matches. In RL mythology, Bradford Bulls were credited with the idea, but it all actually began at Cougar Park. O'Neill and Smith raised the club's playing fortunes and profile, and crowds flocked to Keighley's ground. They snapped up a top coach, Phil Larder, who produced a mesmerising style of play that was a delight to watch. On the cusp of winning the then second division in the 1994-5 season, Keighley signed international stand-off Daryl Powell from Sheffield Eagles, promptly won their league, and then learned they would not be invited to join Super League. The 1995 family boss was as unforgiving as the one a century previously. Keighley kept their nerve for a few more seasons and narrowly failed to get promotion on a couple of occasions, but in the end the dream was unsustainable and the club imploded. Today it sits in the sport's second tier, having just been promoted to the Championship after eight years in the third.

Rugby League is still strongest in the North of England (though there are professional or semi-professional clubs outside the sport's heartlands - two French clubs play in the English leagues, there are two clubs in London, one in North Wales, and one, the latest improbable addition to the RL family, in Cornwall). Rugby League has had the holy grail of expansion in its sights for ever, and many clubs have been established in South Wales, the Midlands, Kent and Gloucestershire, but none have really captured the imagination of the local population to any meaningful extent. London Broncos, established as London in 1981, have had fleeting moments of success (including making it to the Challenge Cup Final in 1998), but have led a nomadic existence and are currently in the second tier. Rugby League is currently in some kind of existential crisis, ironically now dwarfed by the rising financial and media clout of the professional Rugby Union. Instead of talented players from Wales moving north to play Rugby for money, as they did for the first 80 years of the 20th century, they now migrate from League to Union for more money and a higher profile, especially internationally. Jason Robinson became a global superstar when he changed codes and lots of others followed, some with less success. Having said all that, crowds have improved during the 2023 season, with a record established for a round of Super League games over the Easter weekend.

6. A very proud bunch of lads from East Twerton Council School, winners of the Bath & District RFU Cup c. 1905. Postcards like this by local photographers were intended primarily to provide a souvenir for the boys and their families, and the school. I doubt whether many examples of this have survived.

Rugby Union has apparently been expanding very sucessfully since the advent of professionalism, with massively increased crowds, especially for international matches and Premiership games staged at big grounds, but financial issues are beginning to cause headaches. In 2022 two Premiership clubs, Wasps and Worcester, had to withdraw from the competition, and the Welsh regions are undergoing an existential financial and cultural crisis. Meanwhile, in April 2023, RL clubs voted to give marketing group IMG a 12-year contract to 're-imagine' the sport. Their vision ominously excluded automatic promotion and relegation based on playing success from the league structures.

This book is not seeking to chart the history of Rugby in anything other than a superficial way, but rather to show how picture postcards have documented the sport over more than a century.

7. The New Zealand All-Black touring side of 1905 had the status of mythical Gods, but this cartoon published by the Cambridge Picture Postcard Co. portrays them as a devil prior to the tourists playing the University on 9th November 1905 - they won 14-0.

Picture postcards of Rugby Football

The most effective way that personalities, teams and events were portrayed at the start of the 20th century was on picture postcards. I discovered these, like Rugby, almost by accident, spotting some in a collectors' shop on Nottingham's iconic Arkwright Street in the early 1970s. Privately-published picture postcards (as opposed to official Post Office ones) originated in Britain in 1894 and had their 'Golden Age' from c. 1902-18. At that time they were the go-to way of sending brief and urgent messages, the email and social media of their day. Collections and deliveries were frequent and very reliable, so that you could send a message one

8. A fanatical Rugby follower, apparently, on this postcard published by Millar & Lang of Glasgow, posted as a birthday card in May 1910.

morning and be confident it would arrive later the same day (locally) or the next (anywhere in Britain). Postcard publishers used images that represented every type of human activity, including, of course, Rugby Football. Cartoonists had a laugh with incidents and situations in the game, while local photographers recorded town teams, touring sides and individual players. Coverage was random, based on the enthusiasm of particular photographers, so some clubs pop up on postcards frequently and others not at all. The genre fell out of fashion from the 1920s, though postcards of Rugby continued to be issued, and are to the present day. Building a collection of early cards is not easy - many are very scarce - but collectors' fairs, along with specialist and internet auctions, provide a useful potential source.

The cards I've used in this book come mostly from my own collection, though I'm grateful to John Hood for the use of 22 images. The selection is by no means comprehensive, and some readers may be disappointed that their own club or country isn't represented. Pre-1950 postcards on the theme of Rugby are broadly not easy to find, and most early 20th century examples that have survived are now in collections. Finding a specific club team, especially Rugby

9. (left) Smutty was the mascot for the Halifax Northern Union club. This cartoon postcard probably refers to the club's exit from a Challenge Cup campaign.

10. (right) The Leigh NU mascot in 1921, when the club beat Halifax in the Cup Final.

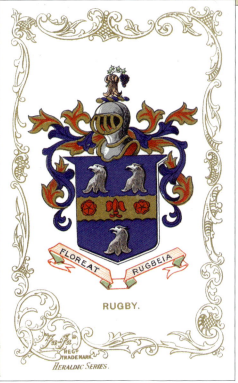

11. (far left) Wakefield Trinity Rugby League player Mick Exley, who won England international caps in the 1930s. He is shown here on this postcard published by Lonnergan of Leeds in the Australia and New Zealand tour jersey of 1936.

12. (left) Halifax firm Stoddart & Co. published pre-1914 hundreds of postcards featuring heraldic crests of towns, cities and universities. This one is for the town of Rugby in Warwickshire, where William Webb Ellis once started a revolution!

Union ones, is tricky, and I haven't come across any early cards of Scottish or French international teams. Because so many Rugby cards are quite scarce, prices are likely to hover between £15 and £40 for photographic examples, and £5-£12 for comic cards.

Thanks to John Hood for the loan of postcards featured as illustrations 23, 34, 100, 106-7, 116-7, 123, 127, 135-7, 145-7, 149-51, 173, 175, 179-80, and for help with information, and to Phil Atkinson for checking the RU captions. Both of them were extremely supportive in encouraging me to complete this project! Thanks also to Michael O'Hare and Geoff Daft for suggesting amendments.

Useful references:
A groundhopper's guide (Mike Latham)
The Book of English International Rugby (John Griffiths)
The Official History of Rugby League (Geoffrey Moorhouse)
Picture Postcard Annual (Reflections of a Bygone Age) provides a listing of postcard collectors' fairs.
Rugby Memorabilia Society publishes a regular magazine (editor Phil Atkinson, akky8@hotmail.co.uk) and books.
Mullock's Auctioneers have regular sales of Rugby memorabilia including postcards.

13. This Wallabies v. Rabbits sketch by N. Parker is obviously some kind of commentary on Rugby opposition for the Australians, though the postcard was apparently published in England and posted at Clifton, Bristol, in December 1905. The Wallabies was the name given to the Australian Rugby Union team that first toured the British Isles in 1908. When a Rugby League team was formed, it was styled The Kangaroos.

14. Anything is possible on postcards! This all-action match between two teams of pigs was painted by Edgar Barnes-Austin as part of a series featuring pigs in various activities. The card was posted at Uckfield in October 1906.

15. Louis Wain was an early 20th century artist specialising in cats and contributed this amazing design. Wain's cats were painted in numerous human situations, and this Rugby scene is one of a number in a series published by Frederick Hartmann of London. It was posted at Leeds in April 1904.

16. These were the Welsh heroes who inflicted the only defeat on the touring All Blacks during their 1905 trip to Britain. The margin was 3-0 but the match probably remains the most illustrious in Welsh Rugby folklore to this day. Each player has a vignette picture on the card, which was published by A. & G. Taylor of London, and posted at Cardiff in January 1906. No reference to the match in the message, though Eric comments "No luck, another chap has got the job".

17. A very early Rugby cartoon, in 'write-away' style, where a simple message was inscribed on the picture side of the postcard for the sender to add to - as on this postard, which was posted at Leeds on 28th December 1901, sent to a Mr Auty in Batley.

The Autograph King

18. A postcard sent by autograph king Reginald Bray. It was posted at Forest Hill, S.E. London, in February 1904 (Bray lived at 135 Devonshire Road) to J.S. Macdonald in Edinburgh, with a request for autograph: *"May I ask you to kindly return this card to the above and add your autograph on the other side, as I want this for my postal collection, thanking you in anticipation"*. Card published by Raphael Tuck, the premier producers of picture postcards in what was their 'Golden Age' (1902-18). James Macdonald of the Edinburgh University side played for Scotland in the international match against England at Inverleith on 19th March that year.

The British Post Office appeared to have been very indulgent with Mr. Bray, giving him two deliveries for one halfpenny!

The way it was, 1904

RUGBY FOOTBALL, A RUSH.

19 and 20. Two examples from a series of six postcards showing various types of incident during a Rugby Union match. The one above is 'A Rush', a term no longer in use but employed in Edwardian days to denote a team chasing after a ball that has been hacked forward. The publisher of the series, Evelyn Wrench, was a postcard entrepreneur who began his business after seeing the popularity of postcards on a trip to Germany and being inspired by the beautiful designs he found there. He published lots of imaginative series, but hopelessly over-reached himself and quickly went bankrupt. The card below shows 'A Scrummage' (or 'Scrimmage' as it was then called), still an integral part of the game of Rugby Union. The scrum has always had its share of controversy as part of the game, in relation to player safety and time consumption. When you analyse it, the contrivance designed to get the ball back into play is a very eccentic one which would never be invented today if it didn't exist. Rugby League recognised many years ago that it was an interruption to the action and sanitised it so that play could resume quickly, allowing in the process a 'feed' by the scrum-half into the second row to make sure that happened. Rugby Union still has a mechanical referee-led process to set a scrum in motion, but now allows feeding, making it almost impossible to lose your own scrum.

RUGBY FOOTBALL, A SCRIMMAGE

Wrench's postcards are based on a match played at Queen's Club, Kensington, which in the early 20th century was a multi-sports facility and later became the headquarters of the Lawn Tennis Association until they sold the premises in 2006. The venue still holds a prestigious annual tennis competition. Teams are London Welsh and Newport (in hoops). The illustrations also feature in a set of Ogden's Guinea Gold cigarette give-aways.

21. The earliest-known Rugby picture postcards published in Britain are a quartet from (probably) 1898, produced by the Pictorial Stationery Co. featuring players from each of the Home Nations. This is the England postcard, showing J.F. Byrne, who played for Moseley and debuted for England at full back in 1894, playing internationals until 1899.

22. Jedforest's J.T. Mabon featured on the Scotland card in the same series. Mabon played fly-half in the 1898 international against England, which ended in a 3-3 draw.

23. In the absence of any other form of quick and inexpensive communication (postcards could be sent for half the letter rate and were delivered reliably quickly), it was common practice until as recently as the 1960s to inform players of selection, or of fixtures for the season, via a postcard. This is a very early example (in fact the earliest known), posted at Greenock on 15th September 1876 and showing the 1876 fixtures for O.H.F.C. (Old Harrovians?). It isn't classed as a picture postcard (privately-produced postcards for use with an adhesive stamp weren't permitted by the Post Office until 1st September 1894) but a postal stationery card with a pre-printed stamp. The list of clubs is interesting - Wasps and Richmond are still going!

24. An artist who signed 'Nap' provided this c.1906 image of a Rugby situation (spot the ball!) on a postcard published by Robert Peel & Co. of Oxford. Numbered 20, it was probably one of a series of sports illustrated by the artist.

Picture postcards of Rugby clubs

Picture postcards were quick to home in on the commercial possibilities of publishing photos of Rugby teams at local and national level from c.1904. Coverage was pretty haphazard, though, and tended to be determined by the enthusiasm of local photographers. Where top clubs such as Newport or Gloucester were concerned, postcards could be marketed to an interested public, but lower down in the hierarchy at the level of village or small town clubs, any postcards that were produced would be largely taken up by players of that club, along with friends and family. In the North of England, there was pretty comprehensive coverage of the professional clubs, with Scott of Manchester leading the way. Cards of amateur RL teams throughout the 20th century are almost impossible to find, though. While the Northern Union quickly adapted the idea of organised leagues, Rugby Union sides played mostly friendlies (apart from County Cups), fixture lists emerging according to playing standards.

A selection of Rugby team postcards appears on the next few pages, the choice being determined by those available from my collection. Below is a quintet of club-supporting badges produced by a firm in Bradford.

Baines club shields

In the late 19th century, John Baines Ltd of Bradford invented the concept of issuing thin paper souvenirs in heraldic shapes supporting a particular Rugby, Football or Cricket clubs. Baines marketed them as being "sought after as eagerly as stamps" and sold them in multiples at one halfpenny a bag. Many included the phrase 'play up'. Shown here are (clockwise from top left) Newport and Moseley (Rugby Union), Keighley, Bramley and Swinton (Northern Union).

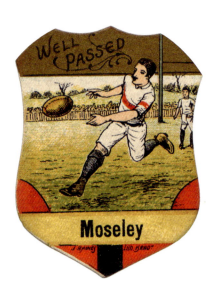

25. Salford Northern Union team in the 1903-4 season. When posting the card in November 1904, the sender noted "This is last year's team, many changes since then".

26. In the same season, but playing a different game, Falmouth RU club became Junior Champions of Cornwall. This card was published by local publisher Harrison from a Cornish Echo photograph. Falmouth, established in 1873, are currently in the 7th tier of English Rugby.

27. French club Perpignan Harlequins in the 1926-27 season on a postcard published by Labouche Bros. of Toulouse.

28. Also from 1903-4 comes this splendid photo of the Newport team of that season. This club was regularly postcarded, partly because there was a prolific postcard publishing firm in the city by the name of Huxtable Bros. The sender of the card (18th April 1904) was, it seems, R.B.G. Lewis (seated left centre) who wrote to W. Clarke in Downpatrick "I hope you will be successful in getting a good pro this season. (excuse me, if this is a reference to Rugby Union, the game was supposed to be completely amateur?) I should like to come back immensely only I am afraid it is impossible... expect if you look hard enough you will find me on the card. This is the Newport XV including some of the injured players. I played centre for the latter part of the season".

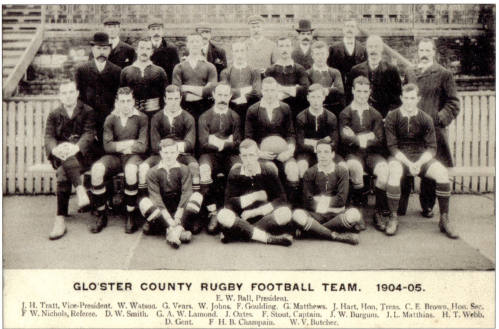

29. Gloucester has always been a hotbed of Rugby Union, and the club is still a leading light in the Premiership. This is their 1904-5 side, and the postcard publishers have helpfully captioned the card with the players' names.

30. How are the mighty fallen! By contrast, the eponymous team Rugby (now called Rugby Lions) have fallen from grace since the onset of professionalism and currently reside in Midlands East One division, the 7th tier of the club game in England. Their ground, Webb Ellis Road, is also umbilically linked to the birth of the game. This postcard flashback to their glory days shows the 1904-5 side, the card published by local photographer Hensman. The card was posted at Sutton Coldfield in September 1905.

31. Many local sports teams in the Edwardian era featured on picture postcards. This is the Kempston (Bedford) team of 1904-5, published by Greenway of Bedford and posted at Kempston in March 1905

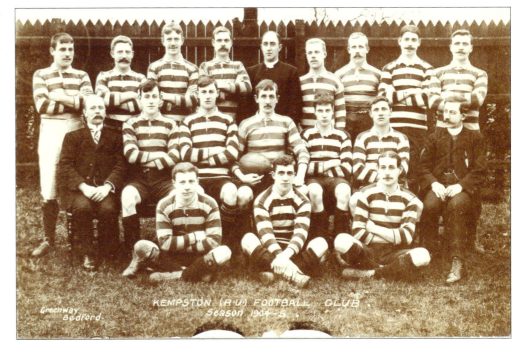

32. A great action shot published by Baxter of Hinckley of the Midlands Cup Final of 1906 between Leicester and Nottingham, played at the Coventry ground.

33. This was an amazingly well-travelled postcard. Published by Leytonstone firm Edwin Walker, it shows the Essex town's Rugby Union team in the 1904-5 season. It was bizarrely posted at Tain, 44 miles north of Inverness, and sent to Miss Argent at Frinton-on-Sea, back in Essex. Walter, who mailed it, wrote: "I don't think you have one of these so thought you would perhaps like one. You will no doubt recognise me". Most of these postcards were, I guess, bought by the players to keep or send to friends.

34. The Llanelly side of 1905-6 season. This famous club was formed in 1872 and played its first match at the iconic Stradey Park ground in 1879. Llanelly have provided 176 international players from their ranks over the years.

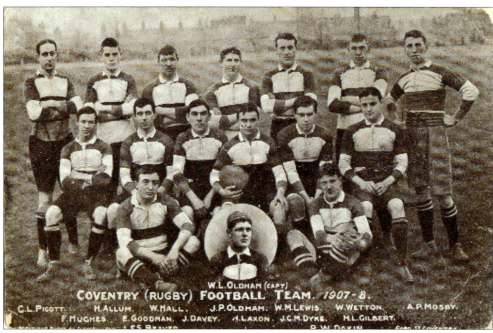

35. Coventry are another club which has fallen from the top tier of English Rugby Union since the advent of professionalism, though not as far as Rugby. Coventry's best years were in the 1960s and 1970s. They are now in the Championship, the second tier. This is their 1907-8 side on a postcard from Jackson & Son of Ford Street, Coventry.

36. The cup-winning Long Buckby (Northamptonshire) team of 1907-8 on an anonymously-published postcard.

37. An action shot during a match between Ilfracombe and Exeter in March 1908. The two clubs are poles apart since Exeter began their rise to the Premiership and European competition.

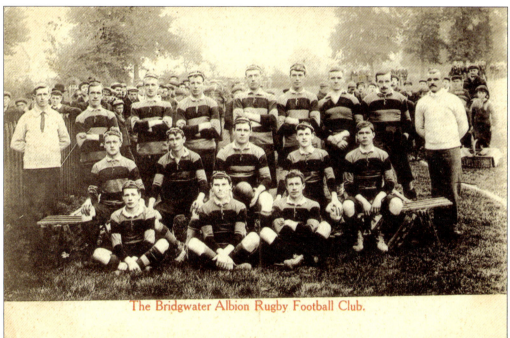

38. This card of the Bridgwater Albion side, formed in 1891, was posted from the town in June 1908. In 1919 the club merged with the older Bridgwater club (founded in 1875) to form Bridgwater & Albion. It is now in the SW1 (west) league in the Rugby Union structure.

39. The sender of this postcard presumably thought he was being helpful in inscribing the names of the Harlequins players on the team picture, but it rather detracts from the image. The card was posted to Drome, France, in March 1908. Publisher was W.S. Stuart of Richmond.

40. Up North, this postcard shows a section of the exclusively male, exclusively flat-capped and mostly moustachioed crowd at a Northern Union match between Barrow and Hunslet in March 1908. It was posted to Douglas, Isle of Man, in the following month.

41. Swinton Northern Union team, formed under Rugby Union rules in 1871, pictured c. 1908. One of the biggest names in Rugby League in the 1920s, Swinton won their first Championship in 1927 and all four available trophies in 1928 - a feat matched only by Huddersfield and Hunslet. Their Station Road ground hosted many RL finals, but the club moved from there in 1992 in controversial circumstances and has been nomadic since.

42. Manchester publishing firm Scott & Co. produced team photos of many Northern Union teams in the mid-Edwardian era. This one features the c.1905 Hull Kingston Rovers side. The club had joined the NU in 1897. Hull KR, known as the 'Robins', are one of two strong sides based in the city. They play in East Hull.

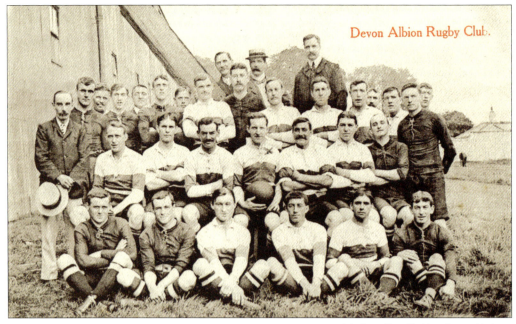

43. Devonport Albion Rugby Union club c.1904. Captain Willie Mills is seated centre with the ball. The card was published by Senior & Co. of Bristol.

44. Bradford's Northern Union team on a Scott-published card c.1904. The club had plenty of success in the 20th century from their base at the iconic Odsal ground - a giant bowl of an arena which boasts the record attendance for a Rugby match - 102,587 for a Challenge Cup replay between Halifax and Warrington in 1954. Anecdotal evidence puts the actual crowd at 125,000+ with many gaining access without being recorded.

Bradford Northern (the name was adopted in 1907) imploded in 1963, but were rescued and re-formed the following year, and then re-incarnated into Bradford Bulls in the Super League era. Initially very successful, the club is now in the second tier after another implosion.

45. Bradford's great rivals have always been near-city neighbours Leeds, seen here c.1905 on another Scott postcard. Founder-members of the Northern Union, Leeds have consistently been one of the leading clubs in Rugby League and have been extremely successful as Leeds Rhinos in the Super League era. They play at another famous ground, Headingley, next door to the Cricket Test Match venue.

OLDHAM R.F.C.

46. Oldham Northern Union team c.1908. Card published anonymously. Oldham have a long and proud history, with plenty of trophies, and were founder members of Super League when that began in 1995. The club slipped quickly down the pecking order, however, and have led something of a nomadic existence since leaving their famous Watersheddings ground. They now reside in the third tier.

47. Wigan is arguably the most famous Rugby League name worldwide. This is their 1904-05 team in the then Northern Union, when they were winners of the West Lancashire Cup. Postcard published by Will Smith of Wigan.

48. Wakefield Trinity Northern Union team at their Belle Vue ground showing off the 1910 Cup. The club still plays at the same ground and is currently upgrading it.

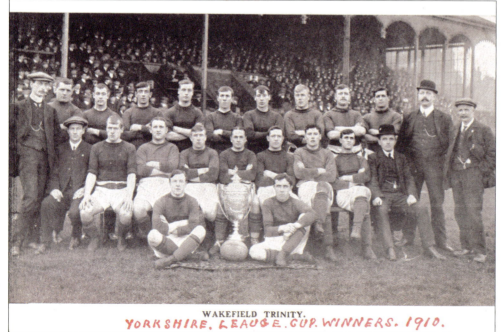

WAKEFIELD TRINITY.
YORKSHIRE. LEAGUE. CUP. WINNERS. 1910.

49. Many North of England sides stayed true to the Rugby Football Union after the 1895 split. Vale of Lune in Lancashire was one of these. This photo shows them in an open field, a big contrast to the previous postcard of Wakefield.

50. Skipton, six miles north of the Northern Union hotbed of Keighley, remained with Rugby Union and won the Yorkshire Cup in the 1911-12 season. This card was published by Skipton photographer Kestin.

51. Carmarthen Harlequins 1911-12 on a postcard published by prolific photgrapher D. Bowen & Son of Haverfordwest and Milford Haven.

52. Dewsbury won the Northern Union Cup in 1912, beating Oldham 8-5 at Headingley, and the team is seen here on a postcard published by Knapton & Co. of Rotherham. Dewsbury joined the NU in 1897, and among the club's highlights since are a victory against the Kangaroos in 1921, an appearance in the first Challenge Cup Final held at Wembley (they lost 2-13 to Wigan in 1929) and a Championship win in 1973.

53. Huddersfield, based in the town that effectively launched what was to become Rugby League, were a powerhouse in the sport for much of the pre-WW2 period, especially the few years before WW1. The club won all four available trophies in the 1913-14 season, when the side included luminaries such as Harold Wagstaff and Albert Rosenfeld. This is their Yorkshire Cup-winning side of 1926-27. More recently, they have been involved in interesting developments. In 1984 they were given the nickname 'Barracudas' (that lasted for four years), were merged with Sheffield in an ill-fated one-season experiment, and were then rebranded as Huddersfield Giants, which they still are today.

54. The Batley Northern Union team of season 1920-21. The club was among the founder-members of the Northern Union in 1895 and won three Challenge Cups in the following six seasons. Playing at Mount Pleasant, Batley, the club is now known as the 'Bulldogs' and is in the Rugby League Championship (second tier).

55. Postcard publisher R. Scott of Manchester included the Ebbw Vale RFC team of 1910 in their portfolio. This club joined the Northern Union in 1907, playing their first match in front of a 4,000 crowd. That season, they played the touring All Gold New Zealanders. Five other clubs from South Wales, which had a similar industrial base to the North of England, joined the NU around the same time, but all folded after early encouraging signs. Ebbw Vale lasted until April 1912. The expansion of Rugby League into South Wales has been tried many times since without lasting success.

56. Bidston Rugby Union club 1920-21 on a card published by W.J. McCullough of Rock Ferry. This no longer exists as a club.

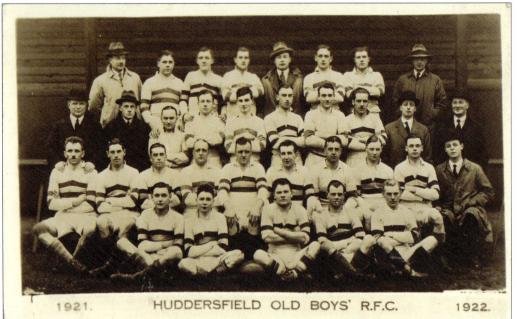

57. All over Rugby League territory, many non-professional clubs existed side by side with their professional counterparts. Many RU sides were based on local Grammar Schools and added an 'Old Boys' reference to their name. This is Huddersfield Old Boys Rugby Union club from the 1921-22 season.

58. Nearby Halifax's Rugby club was founded in 1873 and became one of the breakaway members of The Northern Rugby Football Union in 1895. The club achieved many successes while at its traditional Thrum Hall ground, but recently has had to make do with life in the second tier of the game, the Championship, and now plays at The Shay, groundsharing with Halifax Town FC. This postcard of the 1923-24 team was published by local postcard firm Lilywhite.

59. Plymouth Albion's team of 1927-28. Formed in 1876 by dockyard apprentices, the club had some famous times, including playing a match against the 1905 touring All Blacks (Plymouth lost 3-21), and supplied ten international players in the first decade of the 20th century. They amalgamated with Devonport in 1919, which is when the 'Albion' appendage was added. More recently, the club played in RU's second tier from 2002-15, but went into administration and had to rebuild. Plymouth now play in National League 1.

60. Widnes's first Rugby League Challenge Cup win at Wembley came in 1930 with a 10-3 win against St. Helens, commemorated by this splendid photographic montage postcard by anonymous publisher..

61. This is an unusual postcard in several ways. Firstly, the team group from season 1913-14 has been augmented by non-players and wives or girlfriends; the players are in differing shirts (maybe the photo was taken after a training session?); and, thirdly, Ravensbourne RFC was actually the team set up by the travel company Thomas Cook in 1910 with a ground at Ravensbourne, Beckenham, Kent. Initially known as the Ludgate Circus XV, the Rugby section was part of a wider sports community established by the firm. It developed a wide fixture list against lots of London and south-east clubs. The club name changed to Thos. Cook & Sons RFC in 1926 and it ceased operating in 1966. This postcard dates from the year the First World War began - what happened to all these players in the four years that followed?

62. A postcard published by J. Ingham & Sons of Sale R.U. club's team in the 1931-32 season. Helpfully, postcard publishers tended to inscribe the season featured on the ball held by the captain. Sale are now a powerhouse in the Rugby Union Premiership.

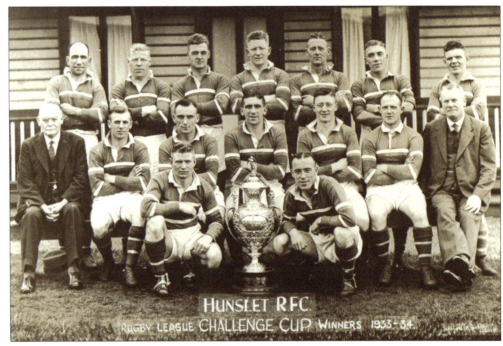

63. The name of Hunslet is a famous one in Rugby League, though the club now languishes in the third tier of the sport's professional and semi-professional structure. This postcard is from its glory days at the old Parkside ground, with the 1933-34 Challenge Cup-winning side shown.

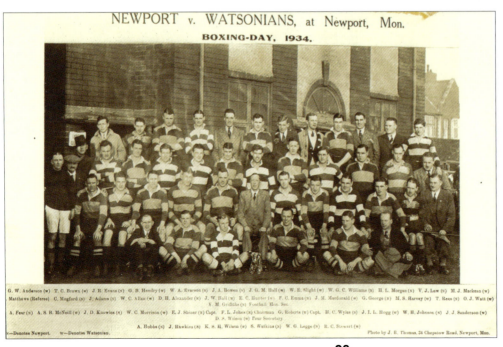

64. The Newport and Watsonians Rugby Union teams from a Boxing Day contest in 1934. The players have interspersed themselves for the photograph, but all the names are printed on the postcard, published by J.E. Thomas of Newport.

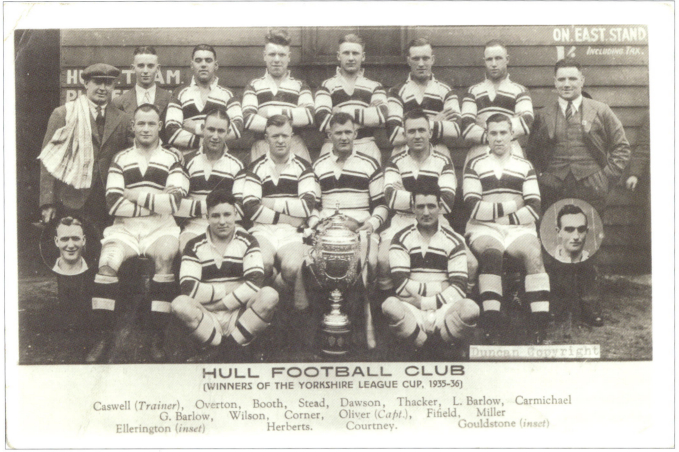

HULL FOOTBALL CLUB
(WINNERS OF THE YORKSHIRE LEAGUE CUP, 1935-36)

Caswell (*Trainer*), Overton, Booth, Stead, Dawson, Thacker, L. Barlow, Carmichael
G. Barlow, Wilson, Corner, Oliver (*Capt.*), Fifield, Miller
Ellerington (*inset*) Herberts. Courtney. Gouldstone (*inset*)

65. When professional Rugby League had only one division, teams effectively played league matches for two trophies. Each played every other side from the same county (Yorkshire or Lancashire/Cumberland) and five sides home and away from the other county. In the 1935-36 season Hull won the Yorkshire competition, winning 23 of their 28 games. This card was published by H. Duncan of Hull.

Back Row: TOWILL HALLIDAY TALBOT J. TRAILL DIXON JONES SHERBURN J. GILL.
Front Row: G. PARKER LLOYD D. M. DAVIES BEVAN HERBERT.

Presented by THE YORKSHIRE EVENING POST.

66. Keighley have reached the Rugby League Challenge Cup Final only once, losing 5-18 to Widnes at Wembley in 1937. This postcard is signed by Joe Sherburn (back row, second from right) and published by the Yorkshire Evening Post. The team had a heavy Welsh contingent that season.

International matches and touring sides

The first overseas Rugby Union team to tour Britain was the 1905 All Blacks, a spectacularly successful team that won 34 of the 35 matches played. Their only loss was to Wales at Cardiff Arms Park, with the home side winning 3-0. This result was an inspiration to postcard publishers in Wales, where the national team instantly acquired iconic status. All the English sides the All Blacks played were defeated, and the tourists beat Ireland 12-7, Scotland and England both 15-0, and France 38-8. The success of the tour encouraged further visits from overseas nations, with a South African party arriving the following year. That side won 26 of its 29 games, losing to Scotland and drawing with England but beating Wales, Ireland and France. The first Australian party (the Wallabies) visited in 1908-9, winning 33 of 39 matches, and beating England 9-3 at Blackheath in the first Test between the two nations. Wales again spoiled the party, beating the tourists 9-6. All three nations returned to tour throughout the 20th century, and recently visits from these three countries - and other Southern hemisphere nations like Argentina and Japan - have become much more frequent.

The Northern Union received its first touring side in 1907 in the shape of the New Zealand All Golds (a sarcastic refence by the NZ RFU to the fact that the players were paid: they still played in black). The RL side later became officially known as the Kiwis. The tourists played 35 matches, including three Tests against the Northern Union, losing 6-14 at Headingley and winning 18-6 at Stamford Bridge, London and 8-5 at, improbably, Cheltenham. Before this, though, the tourists played what was the first-ever Rugby League international, against Wales at Aberdare on New Year's Day 1908. In front of a crowd of 20,000, the Welsh side notched yet another historic win for the country, beating the All Golds 9-8.

Picture postcards of all the touring sides are relatively easy to find, with the 1905 All Blacks, a novelty at the time, especially well featured.

67. A kind of informal photograph of the touring South Africans before their match against Cumberland on 15th December 1906. The match was played at Devonshire Park, Carlisle, and the tourists won 21-0.

68. The legendary New Zealand tourists of 1905, who famously lost only one match on the tour - to Wales. This postcard was published by Millar & Lang of Glasgow.

69. This is the Irish team that played the New Zealand tourists on 25th November 1905, losing 0-15. Card published by Eason & Son of Dublin and Belfast.

70. Devonport Albion played the tourists at The Rectory Ground at Devonport when over 20,000 crammed into the ground to see New Zealand win 21-3. Card published by Scenerique Photo Co.

71. A rare postcard published by Bragg of Illogan, Redruth, showing the 1905 New Zealand tourists on an outing to North Cliffs, Camborne. Nell wrote on the back "I suppose you wanted them in their football cloths (sic.). I sent Dorothy & she brought home these but I suppose you will know them".

72. The 1905 New Zealand tourists were held in high esteem, and this postcard cartoon by artist William Ellam is a kind of devilish tribute to them. The card was published by top London postcard firm Raphael Tuck as 'Souvenir' postcard no. 1429.

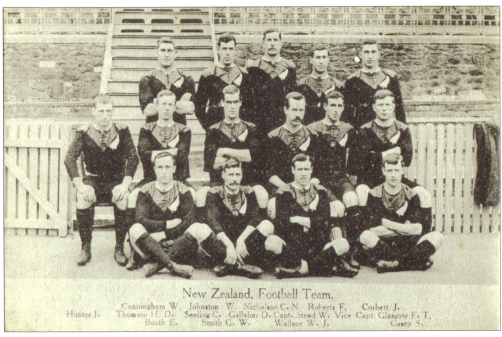

73. As the 1905 New Zealand tourists rolled around the country, local postcard publishers were keen to produce their own cards. This one came from Senior & Co. of Bristol.

74. This postcard was produced by Chas. H. Lewis of Wellington, New Zealand, for NZ supporters to fill in the results of the 1905 tour of Britain and France.

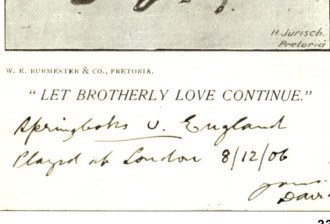

75. W.E. Burmester & Co. of Pretoria published a series of cartoon postcards designed by H. Jurisch for the Springbok tour of the British Isles in 1906. The cards illustrated on this page and following pages were sent to T.J. Cromlin in Edinburgh by someone called David and all were posted in Pretoria nine days after the relevant match. This is the postcard souvenir for the international against England, played at Crystal Palace on 8th December 1906. 40,000 spectators watched a 3-3 draw on a mudbath.

76. The first South African Rugby Union team to tour the British Isles arrived in 1906. This card, published by Senior & Co. of Bristol from a photo taken by Scott of Manchester, shows the touring party in a park (presumably in Manchester), with a watching crowd shoehorned into the bandstand behind and immortalised, like the players, on the postcard.

77. The 1906-07 South African tour of Britain and France was certainly not a walkover, as suggested by the writer on this postcard. The tourists lost to Scotland and drew with England, though they beat Ireland, Wales and France (the latter heavily). This card was posted from Johannesburg on 3rd December 1906 to an address in Fordingbridge, Hampshire, before the England and France matches had been played. The sentiment on the postcard was certainly triumphalist.

78. A postcard with caption in Afrikaans published by the Capetown firm of Townshend, Taylor & Snashall, posted on 5th December 1906 to a G.D. Read of Doncaster, Yorkshire. It is in poor condition (frankly, it is amazing how many postcards have survived in excellent condition over a century later!), but is quite rare and still eminently collectable.

79. This postcard sent on 3rd December 1906 commemorated the international against Ireland, played in Belfast.

80. Souvenir of the match against Scotland, posted from Pretoria on November 26th.

81. The Springboks' 11-0 victory over Wales at Swansea on 1st December (this card was posted nine days later) was represented on this postcard showing the Welsh dragon being unceremoniously dumped over a cliff by a Springbok on horseback.

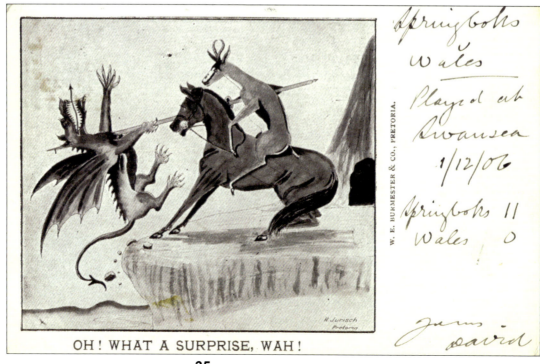

82. Scene from a match at Kingsholm on 1st October 1908 between Gloucestershire and the Australian tourists. Bizarrely, the card wasn't sent until April 1922, when 'Auntie Lena' commented "this photo was taken by Auntie Floss's brother. We have had a heavy fall of snow today & it is so cold".

83. The South African tourists of 1912-13 on a postcard published by Viner of Weston-super-Mare from a photo by Lewis Bros. of Bath. The side won all five Test matches against the Home Nations and France, but lost to Newport, London Counties and Swansea.

84. The East Midlands and South African tourists sides photographed before their match at Northampton in November 1912, which the tourists won 14-5. Postcard published by S.H. Greenway of Northampton.

85. Australian Rugby League tourists were known as the Kangaroos (to distinguish them from the Rugby Union Wallabies). This is the 1929 touring party (the fourth to visit Britain) on a card from Fielding of Leeds. It was posted at Mytholmroyd in January 1930. The hosts won the four-match Test series, and the Kangaroos also lost to Wakefield Trinity.

86. The Springbok tourists of 1931-2. This was the third tour by the South African Rugby Union team to the Northern Hemisphere and resulted in a clean sweep of Test matches. The only team to beat them was an invitational East Midlands team, which won 30-21 at Welford Road, Leicester.

87. An informal photo of the New Zealand Rugby Union tourists of 1935 at their Stratford-on-Avon hotel. Postcard published by Ernest Daniels of the town. The team toured Ireland and Canada as well as Britain, winning 26 and drawing one of the 30 matches they played. The tourists were beaten by Swansea (another scalp for a Welsh club!), Wales and England.

Home Internationals

Today the Six Nations is probably the most prestigious Rugby tournament in the world. Its origins were 152 years ago, when a Scotland national side hosted England at Raeburn Place, Edinburgh, in front of 4,000 spectators. Scotland won 8-3 on a long narrow pitch. England's players were drawn from clubs that no-one today would recognise - West Kent, Gipsies, Ravenscourt Park and Clapham Rovers, along with a couple that have fallen in the pecking order recently - Blackheath and Richmond. The fixture became an annual event and in 1875 Ireland joined the party, with Wales making their international debut in 1881. That didn't go well - England won 56-0 at Blackheath. France, after hosting the New Zealand tourists in 1905, played their first international against England in 1906, losing 8-35 at Parc des Princes in Paris. It was to be another 94 years before the Home Nations tournament was expanded to six when Italy joined in the year 2000.

Picture postcards were not around when these home internationals began, and no images appeared until 1904, when the Scotland-England match was recorded by an Edinburgh optician and postcard publisher. Even then, publishers found the touring sides more interesting and exotic, and more postcards exist of those teams than of the home nations. In fact, cards of the various international teams are not easy to find, with Scotland particularly elusive.

88 to 93. This set of postcards, designed by Paul Pickford, was published by Reflections of a Bygone Age in 2001.

94. An Edinburgh optician turned postcard publisher produced a series of cards featuring the 1904 Rugby Union international between England and Scotland at Inverleith in March 1904. Scotland, captained by prop M.C. Morrison of Royal Herriott's School Former Pupils club, won 6-3, with observers feeling they should have won by more. This postcard was posted at Edinburgh eleven days later and sent to Macclesfield. "Can you spot a few old friends?...Mark Morrison is just behind the Englishman on the right".

95. From the same series, a postcard capturing the ball just after it has been kicked by a Scottish player.

96. A fairly relaxed photo of the 1905 Welsh XV at Swansea (taken by a photographer from Cork, Southern Ireland!). The Welsh won the Triple Crown that year and also hammered England 25-0 at Cardiff Arms Park.

97. The Irish team of 1905 on a postcard published by R. Scott of Manchester, more noted for their Rugby League team photos. They probably obtained the photo from Healey & Sons of Cork, where the international against England was played that year, Ireland winning 17-3. Ironically, man of the match and architect of the Irish victory was Englishman Basil Maclear (third from left, back row, on the photo), a centre, who was stationed in Cork with the British Army and had been rejected as not good enough to play for England.

98. There wasn't much ceremony or formality with team photos in the Edwardian age! Arthur Holborn of Bristol took this photo before the international match against Wales on 18th January 1908, played at Bristol City Football Club's Ashton Gate ground - the only RU international ever played in the city. Wales won 28-18, but many in the crowd missed the majority of the nine tries because of the blanket of fog that covered the ground.

99. A year later Wales won yet again, the eleventh consecutive year that England failed to win this fixture (though the 1904 match was a draw). This 1909 encounter at Cardiff saw Wales succed 8-0. This is the England team for that game; captain was Robert Dibble of Bridgwater Albion.

100. Two for the price of one on this dual-team photographic postcard of the teams before the 1909 Wales - Ireland match played at Swansea. Wales won 18-5 and were Home Nations Championship winners that year.

101. In 1913 England, markedly improved from the previous decade, won the Grand Slam, though lost to the South African tourists at Twickenham in January by 9 points to 3. Their successes in the Five Nations featured wins against Wales (12-0), France (20-0), Ireland (15-4) and Scotland (3-0). Card published by Rees Electric Press of Cardiff.

102. A very ornately-designed postcard, published by J.E. Thomas of Newport, with vignette pictures of the Welsh team that played England at Twickenham on 17th January 1914. Apparently, no photo of the captain, the Rev. Alban Davies, in rugby mode was available, so the publisher used one of him in his day job outfit! Even the inspiration of the churchman captain, who played for Llanelly, couldn't conjure a win for the Welsh, as England edged the match 10-9.

The players

Postcards of individual players are found much less frequently than those of teams, presumably because the sales potential was much less. Coverage was very haphazard, too, though if there was an enthusiastic local photographer such as Duncan of Hull, then plenty of postcards turn up.

Players were much better featured on cigarette cards, so this page provides a diversion from the main theme of the book with a selection of those related collectables.

Centre threequarter Harry Lind played for Scotland from 1928-34, latterly as captain. He played his club rugby for Dunfermline and later London Scottish. State Express 'Sports Champions' series.

From Wills' 'Irish Rugby Internationals' series comes Mick Bradley of the club Dolphins. He also played for his province ("the outstanding forward in Munster Rugger for many years")

R.S. Spong played fly-half for England in 1929-30. He starred for Old Millhillians and Hampshire, too. Lambert & Butler's 'Footballers 1930-1' series.

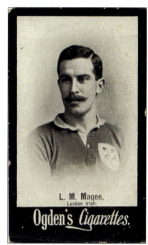

L.M. Magee of London Irish on an Ogden's-issued cigarette card.

Leeds Rugby League player Stanley Brogden (he also played for Bradford Northern and Huddersfield) was the first Rugby player to be transferred for £1,000. He scored ten tries in his first match for Bradford. Card from Ogden's 'Football Caricatures' series - no artist acknowledged.

Ivor Jones of Llanelly and Wales in Lambert & Butler's 'Footballers 1930-1' series.

J.H. Harris of Canterbury in Wills' 'New Zealand Footballers' series

T. Lawton was an Australian who played for Oxford University and Blackheath, and had a trial for England, being named as reserve fly-half. This is from F & J Smith's 'Prominent Rugby Players' series.

103. 'Whacker' (Charles Albert) Smith of Gloucester on a postcard published by the Royal Standard Photo Co. of Evesham and sent to Master Charlie Printer of Prestbury Farm, Bulley, near Gloucester, in March 1907. Whacker played for the club from 1897-1908, a fearsome tackler on the wing. He played once for England, against Wales in 1901.

104. Frank 'Patsy' Boylen was a dual-code international, playing for England in both Union and League. He was born in Hartlepool and played for both the town's sides before turning professional with Hull Kingston Rovers in 1909. This postcard, signed by the player, was published by Duncan of Hull.

105. You might not guess it, but these are Northern Union players and club officials from Hull F.C. out on a motoring jolly. Seated with pipe in mouth is Australian import Steve Darmody, who joined Hull after he had toured with the 1911-12 Kangaroos. He played for the club as a goalkicking winger from 1912-14, and then enlisted in the British Army on the outbreak of war.
Card published by Duncan of Hull.

106. (right): J.W. Brough played for Cumbrian side Silloth and won two international caps with England in 1925, playing against New Zealand and Wales at Twickenham

107. Gwyn Nicholls won 24 Welsh caps as a centre. He played most of his career (1891-1906) with Cardiff, captaining them for five seasons during that time. He was known as the 'Prince of threequarters' and Cardiff Arms Park has memorial gates dedicated to him. Nicholls was captain of the Welsh side that defeated the All Blacks in 1905.

108. Postcarded Rugby players were normally high-profile ones, but I'm not aware that W. Lindsay Beattie was famous. He played for Blackhill RFC (now Consett) in Co. Durham. At any rate he autographed this postcard for a friend or fan.

109. A couple of Welsh internationals in 1929 appeared on this anonymously-published postcard. Guy Morgan, a centre, played for the Swansea club and captained his country. Frank Williams made 14 appearances for Wales and at club level played for Cardiff, Wakefield and Headingley.

110. (right) Hull F.C.'s Australian wing Steve Darmody - a signed postcard published by Duncan. Darmody scored six tries in his 89 appearances for Hull.

111. Wakefield Trinity and England Rugby League player H. Kershaw personally inscribed this postcard, published by the Black & White Studios of Wakefield.

112. Rugby League player M. Lavelle made his debut for York in September 1907. He played 148 games for the club in the next six seasons, scoring 29 tries and 7 goals.

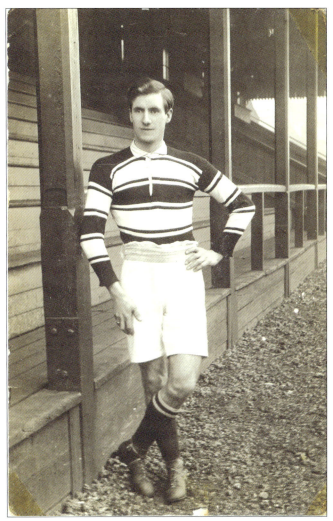

113. Hull's John (Jack) Harrison played five games for York before joining Hull F.C., for whom he made 116 appearances, scoring 106 tries from the wing position. During the First World War he became an officer in the British Army and won the Victoria Cross posthumously for special gallantry.

114. Joe Hamill of Hull and previously Dewsbury Northern Union clubs in the period 1912-17.

115. Duncan of Hull published this postcard showing Hull F.C. legend and utility back Billy Batten at The Boulevard (the club's ground until 2003, when they used the new Kingston Communications Stadium in conjunction with the city's football club), with his son Billy junior on horseback. Batten also played for three other Yorkshire clubs along with Great Britain and Yorkshire. He made 226 appearances for Hull, scoring 89 tries.

Rugby's County Championships

For Rugby Union, the County Championship, initiated in 1889, was a big deal, providing a competitive structure in an era of amateurism. It is still played for today, though the top players are no longer eligible, and it has three different tiers for players at varying levels. The top competition was renamed in 2017 in honour of ex-England international Bill Beaumont.

At the start the structure was extremely haphazard, with the competing teams not playing the same opponents, and an RFU panel weighed up the winner! For four years from 1891 it was played for in regions, with the respective winners slugging it out to decide the champion county. North and South regions only were established in 1896, but it was upped to five regions from 1921, followed by semi-finals and a final. The advent of professionalism in Rugby Union changed the situation in that clubs did not want their highly-paid employees being injured in friendly matches. Even so, the competition has retained the loyalty and interest of lots of fans. Over its 133 years (though with no competition in the war years), Lancashire have been the most successful county with 25 titles, followed by Gloucestershire (17) and Yorkshire (15). Five-figure crowds were recorded for many pre-1984 Finals (in that year, the venue was established as Twickenham) at grounds as diverse as Carlisle, Blundellsands and Blaydon.

The County Championship has been particularly well-supported in Cornwall, especially more recently. Six of the county's seven titles have come since 1991, and they are the current holders of the trophy. Their other success was in 1908, when Durham were defeated 17-3 at Redruth, a result that led to Cornwall being invited to compete in the London Olympics that year.

The Northern Union and Rugby League have also had their own County Championship (from 1895-1983 except in wartime), mostly involving just Yorkshire, Lancashire and Cumberland/Cumbria. As with the RU competition, Lancashire have won the most titles. I have not seen any picture postcards relating to the RL version.

116. This postcard of the Devon County team of 1907 includes, front left, James Peters, the first black man to play for England. Peters was born in Salford in 1879, lost his father when he was nine, was abandoned by his mother, joined a circus and was thrown out of it when he broke an arm, and ended up in an orphanage in Greenwich, still only 11. James excelled at sport, and by the time he'd learned the carpentry trade and moved to Bristol, he was snapped up by two junior clubs and then Bristol. Between 1900 and 1903 he represented Somerset till he moved further south and played for Plymouth and Devon. A brilliant fly-half, he nevertheless faced plenty of discrimination, including from the 1906 touring South Africans, some of whom refused to play against him, and all of whom refused to be photographed with the Devon team while Peters was in it. He was picked to play for England against Scotland in the 1906 game (England won 9-3) and played one other game that year (but was not picked to play against South Africa) and three more in 1907-8. Then in 1912 he was suspended for accepting payments to play from Devon RFU. Disillusioned with the RU game, he moved North to play for Barrow and later St. Helens in the Northern Union. It was to be a further eight decades before another black man represented England RU, when winger Chris Oti made his debut in the Scotland match in 1988. Before that, however, Clive Sullivan made history as the first black man to captain a British national side - the Great Britain Rugby League team that won the World Cup in 1972.

117. Somerset's team c. 1908. The county side won the title in 1923, beating Leicestershire 8-6 at Bridgwater Albion's ground.

118. Contesting the ball at a line-out in the Devon v. Durham County Championship match at Exeter in 1907. The postcard was posted at West Hartlepool - in September 1907 - and sent to Gosforth. "Will turn out on Sat", promised the sender, presumably in a reference to his availability for a rugby match.

119. For Cornwall rugby followers, the County Championship was a focal point in their identity, and local postcard publishers produced souvenirs at every opportunity. This one came from A.E. Belletti of Falmouth, and featured the county side that beat Devon 21-3 at Redruth on 13th February 1908. Team was (back row): Tregwrtha, Wilson, Jackson, Mitton, Thomas, Jackett (centre): Lawry, Bennatts, Jackett, Solomon, Jose, Dean (front): Davy, Davey, Wedge.

120. 1908 was most definitely Cornwall's golden year. As well as winning the County final, beating Durham 17-3 (action from the game shown on this postcard published by S.J. Govier of Chacewater, a noted Cornish postcard publisher), they represented England at the Olympic Games later that year, losing to Australia in the only match played in the tournament. England declined to enter a national team on the ground the team was insufficiently prepared!

121. The Lancashire county side in the 1911-12 season. The backs are indicated by the use of the appropriate fraction numeral or the word 'back'. The forwards are not given the same specific treatment, though. Postcard published by J. Cleworth of Greenheys.

122. Posted at St. Day in January 1914, this postcard has a scene from a county match between Cornwall and Gloucestershire in the 1913-14 season.

123. Cheshire's 1922 county side. That year Gloucestershire beat North Midlands 19-0 in the Final. Cheshire's first success in the competition came in 1950, when they beat East Midlands 5-0 in the Final at Birkenhead Park.

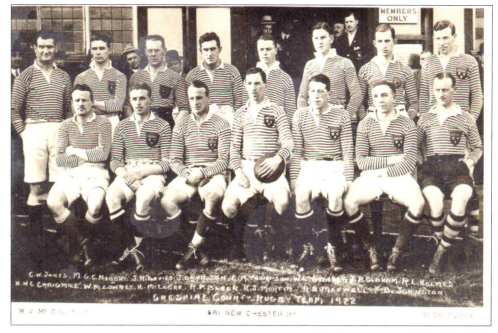

124. A postcard pubished by F.W. Tassell of Carlisle featuring the County Championship-winning Cumberland team of 1924. Back (l. to r.): J. McCade (Keswick), R. Harvey (Aspatria), H. Wills (Kendal), E. Valentine (chairman, from Workington), J. Ward (Aspatria), J. Brough (Silloth), E. Cass (Rhine Army), A.W. Angus (referee, Scottish Society). Front (l. to r.): W.H. Walling (Kirkby Lonsdale), T. Cavaghan (Carlisle), T. Little (Workington), T. Lawson (Workington), T.E. Holliday (Aspatria), R. Lawson (Workington), B.H. Tucker (Carlisle), J. Little (Workington), W. Burrows (Workington). Cumberland won the Final at Carlisle 14-3.

125. Runners-up Kent in that final, played on 5th April 1924. The referee also pops up on this card! While the names of the Cumberland side were helpfully inscribed on the back of the above postcard, Kent's team was not similarly captioned. Tassell also published this postcard.

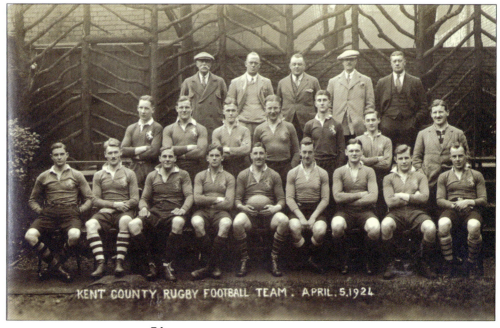

Rugby art on picture postcards

Like other sports, Rugby became a focal point for artists and illustrators, often portraying the game in humorous form. Lots of examples of artist-drawn postcards are scattered through the book, but this section provides an interesting selection. Artistic licence is evident in many of the paintings.

126. An intriguing painting on this postcard of what is obviously a game of Rugby in progress, though the posts have been carelessly drawn! They are too high for a football net, yet the upper part of each upright has been omitted. No artist or publisher is credited on the card.

Front cover of a yearbook for the Northern Union, the last year before the name was changed to Rugby League. The publication included the fixtures of the 26 professional clubs then in business (most are still operating, though Bramley, Broughton Rangers and St. Helens Rec. have folded). Also featured are the fixtures for the touring Australians for 1921-22, the laws of the game, league and cup winners for the previous season and pen-pictures of leading players.

127. A French-published postcard showing a line-out situation, designed by an artist called Boby. Spot the current penalty offence here!

128. This postcard was also published in France, and the artist was also French. His real name was Charles Edmond Hermet, but he wanted to Anglicise himself and took the pseudonym Harry Eliott. His art deco take on a rugby match makes for a fine picture.

129. A leather-bound rugby ball houses 12 miniature pictures of Prees Heath military camp and surrounding villages, revealed when the flap at the top of the ball is detached. These 'novelty pull-out' postcards were popular pre-1914. This one was published by Photochrom of London and Tunbridge Wells. 'Rugger' remained a common way to refer to the game of Rugby Union until relatively recently; indeed, it survives today in the R.F.U.'s fun programme for tots, 'Little Ruggers'.

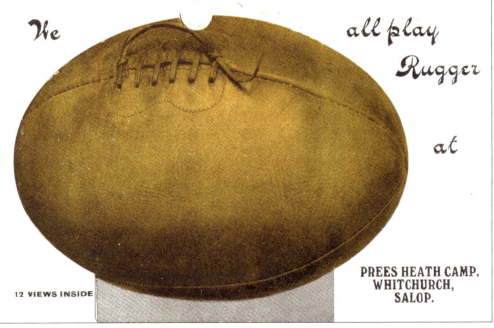

130. This postcard is in poor condition,
having been creased across the centre (see top picture) but is nonetheless
interesting because it is another one that Reginald Bray mailed (see p.2 and p.10). Bray was seeking an autograph from David Bedell-Sivright, who had been appointed captain for the summer's British Lions tour of Australia and New Zealand. He initially posted this card at Forest Hill, South-east London, on 20th March 1904, addressing it to Cambridge University, where the player was studying. It arrived the following day, but the postcard missed him - he was back in Edinburgh. The card was returned to Reginald at 135 Devonshire Road, Forest Hill, whereupon he redirected it to North Queensferry with his usual request. Bedell-Sivright duly signed it on 7th May. Bray certainly got a good deal from the Post Office with the double and sometimes treble mailing of each postcard for a one-halfpenny stamp! The postcard was published by Raphael Tuck in their 'Oilette' series of 'Football Incidents'. The picture, painted by C.M. Padday, shows a scene in an Oxford-Cambridge Varsity match, an appropriate subject for the required signature. Sivright broke his leg on tour, briefly settled in Australia, but was back to lead Scotland against the touring New Zealanders in 1905. He died of septicaemia while working as a naval surgeon in the Gallipoli campaign of 1915.

131. A Christmas greetings theme postcard, published by W. Hagelberg of London and New York, with a rugby theme: 'You've my best wish, in life's rough play, To come out top, in every way'.

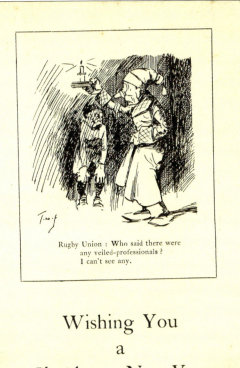

132. The year of issue of this New Year postcard is unclear, but the cartoon's reference to 'veiled professionals' (Rugby Union players accepting money for playing in contravention of the strict amateur regulations) is interesting.

133. Another postcard in the series published by Hagelberg, with a bridge card game reference.

134. 'Grand Slam' is a term used in Tennis, Rugby and Baseball to denote 100% records in specific competitions. Pretty impressive scrum here!

Rugby at The Olympics

Rugby Union's presence at the Olympic Games has been very limited, with the sport being included only in 1900, 1908, 1920 and 1924. The Sevens version of the game was admitted to the Summer Olympics in 2016. Rugby League has never made it, despite strenuous efforts. Rugby was dropped after the 1924 Olympics in Paris, where only three nations - United States, France and Romania - competed. The final match, which the United States unexpectedly won 17-3, was marked by violent behaviour from a very partisan French crowd.

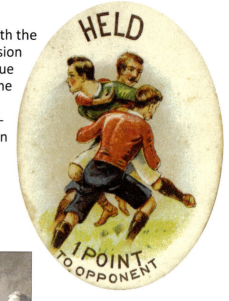

135. Prior to 2016, the last time that Rugby Union had appeared at the Olympic Games was 1924. This souvenir postcard shows the French team.

136. The U.S.A. team beat Romania 37-0 before springing an upset on the host nation.

137. A fine action shot from the France-Romania match at the 1924 Olympics, when the French won 59-3.

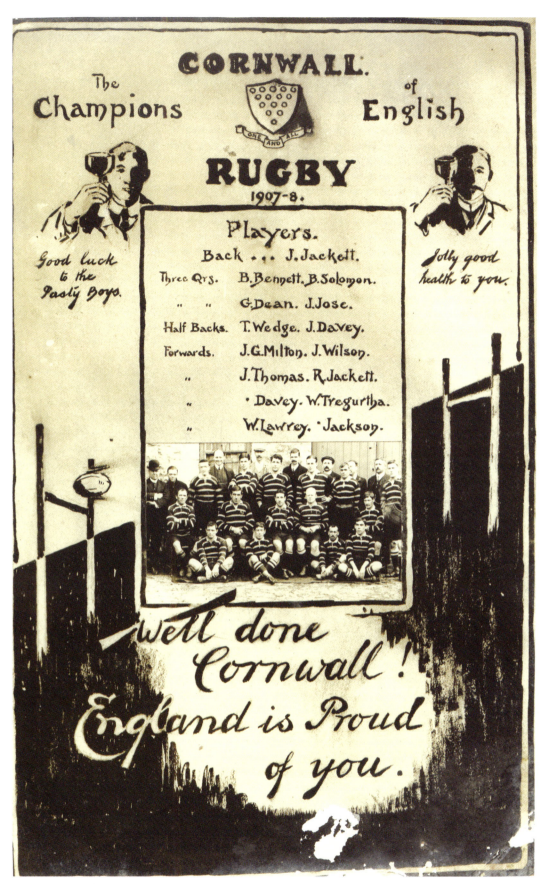

138. Cornwall's Olympic year! When France and Great Britain pulled out of the 1908 Olympic Games Rugby Union tournament in London, and England apparently couldn't field a side, Cornwall were invited, as County Champions, to represent the country. The only other entrant was Australia, who ran out 32-3 winners in the tournament's only match on a seriously bad weather English afternoon.

Grounds and games

Postcards of Rugby matches in action in the Edwardian period are not that easy to find, hardly surprising given the tricky nature of sports photography at the time. It was complicated enough taking still photographs, never mind when the tableau was moving! Where you do find them, the cards are often unlocated. Even photos of grounds are few and far between pre-1980. Postcard publishers found it easier to take still photos of teams or players, where there was a ready market among the participants, friends and family.

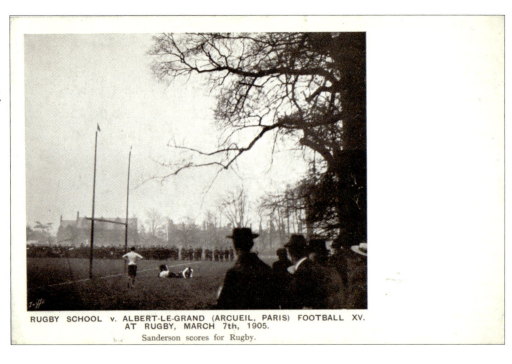

139. A match at Rugby School, where it all started, against a team from Paris in 1905.

140. A great study of a Rugby Union match. The caption suggests this picture was taken at West Hartlepool, but the card was posted at Argoed in Monmouthshire and sent to a local address, with no comment on the picture, and in fact it is Rodney Parade, Newport, with the Durham side the visitors. It was considered polite at the time to give the name of the visiting side first (and on programmes), unlike the convention today. Card published by Huxtable Bros.

141. Action from an Army Rugby (Union) Cup match in 1913 between the 2nd Life Guards and the Somerset Light Infantry.

142. Blake & Edgar were top postcard publishers in Bedford, and one of their series illustrated Rugby Union being played at the town's Grammar School. This example was posted from Kempston to Edgbaston in March 1906.

143. A big crowd is in evidence at the match between Birkenhead Park and Hull & East Riding on 26th March 1921. The photographic scene was published by W. McCullough of Rock Ferry.

144. A much lower key occasion shown on this postcard of a match in progress at the Fylde club. Card published by J.R. Wright of Ansdell.

145. Rugby at Toulouse c.1905 on a postcard published locally. In France, the custom was to stick the stamp on the front of a card.

146. Rugby at Toronto University, possibly in the 1920s. The city was the location in 2017 for another instalment of Rugby League's expansionist dreams. A team called the 'Toronto Wolfpack' was formed (comprising virtually all English and Australian players rather than home-grown ones) and rose from the sport's third tier to Super League before collapsing during the Covid pandemic amid a financial crisis.

147. A French postcard published by Neurdein with the caption 'an unavoidable tackle'. Location unknown.

148. Though uncaptioned, this postcard published by the Leeds Mercury is said to be a scene at Headingley Rugby Union Club's ground in the 1920s.

149. French Championship Final action on 4th April 1909. The teams were Toulouse and Bordeaux, the caption suggesting that a Toulouse 'dribble' (kicking the ball forward in short bursts by the pack as a unit, a tactic that was still regularly employed up to the 1960s) has just been halted by the Bordeaux team. Postcard in a series published by Labouche Bros. of Toulouse.

150. And yet more action from the same match - the ball has just been thrown in at a line-out.

151. Another card in the same series - the ball comes free after a maul.

152. Grassroots Rugby somewhere! The game is played by people of wildly differing standards and ability, and this postcard, published by the Northern Echo newspaper, shows a serious fun match c.1924. Location is probably close to Darlington, where the paper was published.

153. In contrast, this location is the tops of Rugby Union in England. This is the Twickenham ground, but not as you know it. This postcard shows an assembly of Jehovah's Witnesses in July 1955.

154. A French postcard, published by Neurdein, in a 'Sports' series, showing a Rugby scrum during a match at an unidentified location.

155. The Wanderers ground in Johannesburg, a multi-sports complex that has hosted many RU internationals. The card was published by Sallo Epstein of Durban, a famous South African postcard firm, and posted to Market Harborough, Leicestershire, in January 1909.

156. Rugby Union at St. Bees Grammar School in Cumbria c.1905.

157. Plymouth Football ground on a postcard published by Valentine of Dundee c.1906.

158. The Ley's College ground at Cambridge on a postcard published by Henri Moss & Co. of London and posted from Cambridge to Norton-on-Tees in October 1905.

159. Cardiff Arms Park in the 1960s on a postcard published by Francis Frith of Reigate. The ground was one of Wales' venues for staging internationals from 1893 - others were Newport's Rodney Parade, Llanelli's Stradey Park, and St. Helen's Swansea - but Cardiff Arms Park was used exclusively from 1954 until the building of the Millennium Stadium. The pitch at the Arms Park is now at right-angles to the picture here.

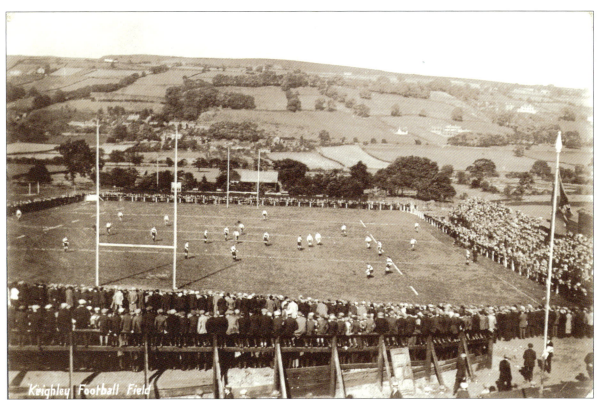

160. One of England's most scenic Rugby grounds, Keighley's Lawkholme Lane has been a venue for Rugby League since the 19th century. Set at the eastern end of the town in the Aire Valley, it is still close to open countryside, though stands have been erected on two sides of the ground since this photographic postcard was published in the late 1920s by Lilywhite of Halifax and posted to Ilkley in June 1930. The ground was renamed 'Cougar Park' in 1992 when Keighley rebranded the club as 'The Cougars' and launched a glorious three years, only for the venture to end in tears in 1995 when Keighley were unjustly denied admission to the newly-formed 'Super League'.

Turning politics into Rugby

Picture postcards permeated every area of life, and political comment and satire was widespread in the early 20th century. Cartoonists often used sporting allegories to illuminate an issue, and Rugby features in this selection, four of which were published in France. Other examples using other sports include a set showing British Edwardian politician Joseph Chamberlain playing cricket (with political references) and numerous examples of the First World War compared to a football match, sometimes involving the use of the Kaiser's head as a ball. Postcards could be very important in influencing the thinking of the public, making them possibly more significant than newspapers, where cartoons had a very temporary shelf life.

161. In the Autumn of 1914, on the outbreak of the First World War, postcard firm Bamforth of Huddersfield, later best known for their cheeky seaside comics, commissioned their staff artist Douglas Tempest to design a series of 'War Cartoons' lampooning German Emperor Kaiser Wilhelm II. No. 54 in the series featured an imagined Rugby match, where the referee was chiding Wilhelm for his bullying of a Belgian player, a reference to the German invasion of that country in August 1914.

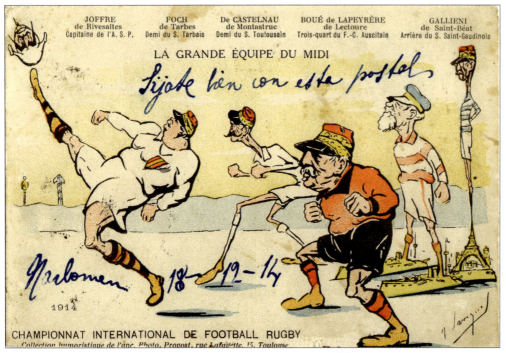

162. Above: another First World War Rugby allusion on this postcard published by Valentine of Dundee, with a German soldier optimistically hoping for a favour from Uncle Sam. The Americans' entry into the war in 1917 was very important in changing the course of it.

163. Left: posted on 21st December 1914 at Narbonne, this French postcard envisions the First World War as a Rugby encounter, with French generals featured in the cartoon. Joffre is giving the German Kaiser Wilhelm II a good kicking.

164. French artist T. Bianco saw French politics as sporting rivalries between competing personalities and produced a series of postcards, 'Football Présidential a Versailles' to make the point. On this card, 'Before', the Presidential election is being tossed to a bunch of candidates as a rugby ball.

165. 'During' the election, the candidates engage in a rough and tumble scramble for votes, represented by the ball.

Presumably, there is at least one other postcard in the series, 'Apres', but I have yet to find it - the appeal of postcard collecting is partly the search for the elusive. I'm guessing this series is extremely scarce, but French collectors might beg to differ!

166. Another political comment on a French postcard. Raymond Poincaré was Prime Minister of France from 1926-29, and on this cartoon carries the French nation in his safe hands as a rugby ball.

Advertising with Rugby

The nature of advertising is such that manufacturers and businesses have always sought connections with popular culture, especially sport, in order to make whatever they are supplying more attractive to consumers. Today that has reached saturation point with Rugby clubs at all levels maximising their income by looking for more and more sponsor advertising. Rugby jerseys, once a statement of a club's identity, have become a blur of sponsors' names, logos and artwork (along with shorts, socks and everything else worn by players!). Ground perimeter and programme advertising has also proliferated remorselessly. Picture postcards can be found on the advertising/Rugby theme over the past 125 years, with a selection included here.

167. Nottingham printers Hamel & Co. published calendars in postcard form from 1905-12, each year featuring a different theme and 12 related images. The subject for 1908 was 'Imps' and October's card showed a Rugby match in progress. Reverse text stated: 'Our present increasing trade is in perfect harmony with our established system in making each order a stepping stone to success'.

168. The Hotel Bonnard Alexandrie in Paris (now just the Alexandrie) published a series of 12 postcards in the early 20th century to advertise its facilities. This is no. 9, captioned 'Football', though obviously showing a Rugby match.

169. The Royal Agricultural Showground, Sydney, hosted a Test match between Great Britain and Australia on 18th June 1910, won 27-20 by GB. The tour was the first by the Lions Rugby League (Northern Union) team and included matches in New Zealand. The Sydney Test, watched by 42,000, also featured a goal-kicking competition between the two sides' respective captains, Dally Messenger of Australia and Jim Lomas, which the latter won 3-2. Sydney firm Nicholson & Co. used the picture on an advertising postcard.

170. A 1980s postcard advertising the restaurant at the rugby club (sic: lower case) in London run by ex-England Rugby Union international Jeff Butterfield and his wife Barbara for 25 years. This example was posted to a prospective client in August 1985.

171. Frank Sugg Ltd of Liverpool manufactured sports equipment, so an advertising postcard featuring Football was an obvious choice in an era when picture postcards were a popular advertising medium. Rugby is allocated a minor place on this design, but at least it's there! This postcard was sent from Wednesbury in January 1911. The message confirms a league match at Football between Darlaston and Wednesbury the following Saturday.

Having a laugh with the game

Cartoons have been a staple and prominent part of the picture postcard industry since its emergence in the late 19th century. In Edwardian Britain artists who were satirists, cynicists and social observers competed to have their work featured on postcards. Some, like Tom Browne, Lance Thackeray, Donald McGill and Louis Wain, all household names at the time, were credited on the designs because their names sold the product. Others' work was produced anonymously, their publishers obviously seeing them as useful contributors but paying them less. During the Golden Age of Postcards, just about every facet of human life was covered and Rugby was no exception. Its characters, game situations, cultural norms and foibles were all laid bare in an explosion of design and promotion. Specific characters were rarely depicted on comic cards, though J.M. Staniforth's Welsh series featured actual clubs. Most common cartoon scenes showed incidents during the match - scrums, tackles, try-scoring, referees and injuries. Some series picked up on the game's phrases - 'kick-off', 'held up on the line', 'time' - and found sketches unrelated to Rugby to illustrate them.

     Edwardian comic postcards didn't lean specifically towards Rugby Union or the Northern version, but I'm assuming that most were based on the original version of the game, given that most of the artists and publishers involved were based in either London or Glasgow. Comic Rugby cards from Yorkshire or Lancashire publishers are very seldom seen.

     Comic postcards were generally issued by publishers in sets of six, though Rugby-focused designs were sometimes only one or two of such sets. Glasgow publishers Millar & Lang were strongest in their promotion of whole sets based on the sport.

172. Tom Browne (1870-1910) was a famous Edwardian cartoonist who designed specifically for picture postcards, most of which were published by London firm Davidson Bros. This one comes from a series illustrating a popular contemporary catchphrase. This example was posted in 1905.

173. J.M. Staniforth was a well-known cartoonist with the Western Mail newspaper and contributed a number of designs in the postcard medium. Perhaps his most sought-after cards are those on Rugby, showing Welsh players of specific teams in cartoon action. Pictured right is his Welsh international offering.

174. 'Are we downhearted?' was a popular Edwardian catch-phrase, used on this Cardiff card. At the bottom is an extra message. The card was posted at Newport in May 2015, sent to Northampton.

175. Penygraig are no longer one of the household names of Welsh Rugby, but in 1908 this small village in the Rhondda Valley had a side so good it was awarded a fixture against the visiting Wallabies. Staniforth designed a postcard for each of the Welsh sides that played the tourists. Penygraig, which at this time provided some Welsh internationals, lost 3-11 but with a very decent performance.

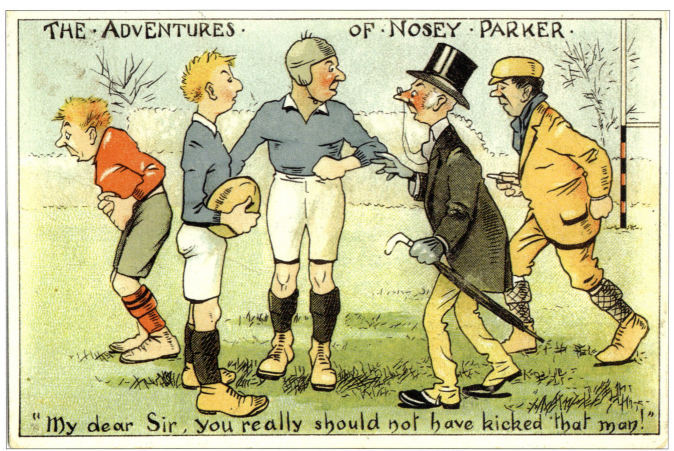

176 and 177. No artist is credited on this pair of comic postcards - part of a set of six, of which only two feature Rugby - but it is possible they were designed by the great Donald McGill, 'King of the seaside postcard'. The Nosey Parker character interfered in things that were none of his business in the series, and on the second card here he receives his come-uppance. The postcards were produced by the Regent Publishing Co. of London, and the top one was posted at Mountain Ash in July 1909.

178. The three postcards on this page are definitely McGills. This is one of his very earliest - he designed cards from 1904-62, a pretty impressive career achievement, and a number of his designs had Rugby themes. He seems to have been a big fan of the game, despite having a foot amputated after an injury sustained in a game at Blackheath Preparatory School. This one was published in the 'Empire' series by Hutson Bros. of London and posted at Maldon in April 1906.

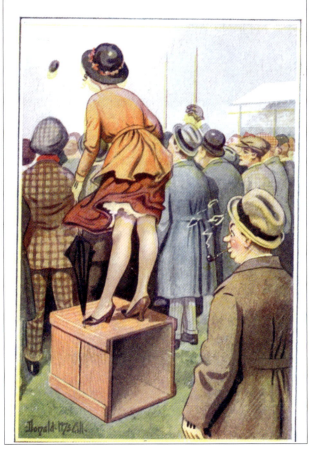

179. A typical McGill innuendo on this postcard published by the Inter-Art Co. in the 1930s

180. An early c.1910 McGill cartoon published by Joseph Asher & Co.

181. Another McGill offering, published by the Inter-Art Co. of London in their 'Comique' series and posted at Northampton in October 1923.

182. I'm not sure this tackle would find favour with the Rugby authorities in 2023. The postcard, published by Millar & Lang of Glasgow, was sent in August 1908, addressed to the captain of the football team, South Brent: "Hope you won't get held in such a tight embrace".

183. Published by Woolstone Bros. in their 'Milton' series, this is McGill's take on the egg-like shape of a rugby ball.

184. Glasgow publishers Millar & Lang produced a series of six postcards showing interpretations of words or phrases used in Rugby. Three of them are shown on this page. Right is 'Kick off', with a prospective suitor being given the boot by a girl's father. It was posted from London in February 1904.

185. 'Time' was posted on the same day to the same address, the message being a continuation of the previous card, a discussion about the prevailing extremely windy weather.

186. 'Held up on the line' was illustrated by a robbery on a train track. This postcard was posted at Swinton, Lancashire (a famous old Rugby League town), in June 1904.

187. Typical example of a 'write-away' postcard, popular in the early 20th century, where a useful phrase, which could be completed or added to by the sender, was used as the caption. 'I hope you will join us...' could have served as a party invitation. Before January 1902, any message had to be written on the picture side of a postcard as the back was used exclusively for the address. 'Undivided back' cards, as they were known, continued to be used long after the Post Office allowed a message on a 'divided back' postcard.

188. Another card in the same series, which was published by Ernest Nister, a prominent postcard firm based in Nuremberg, Germany, but with an office in London. The artist's initials were E.S.H., but beyond that I cannot identify the full name. The card above was posted from Exeter to Cricklewood in October 1904, this one from Margate to Chiswick in August 1905.

189. A postcard from Millar & Lang c.1905. 'A Mark' is a Rugby Union term indicating a clean catch effected within the 25-yard (22-metre) line, but in this instance the artist gives it another twist.

190. More cards from Millar & Lang on this page, two of them illustrating match situations. This one shows an early try-diver in the style now favoured by all wingers.

191. A tough kid showing the scars of battle, but still a hero. This card was posted at Hadfield, Derbyshire, in October 1908.

192. A feeling that every full-back has faced is encapsulated on this cartoon. The card was posted from South Brent to Ivybridge in August 1908.

193. Women's Rugby originated in the 1880s, but on a very small scale, with just a few exhibition games. A charity match between Cardiff Ladies and Newport Ladies (6-0 to Cardiff) took place in December 1917. It wasn't until the 1960s that the game really began to grow significantly. It is currently amazingly successful, with a full Six Nations programme, an elite league in England, and lots of grass-roots Rugby. This postcard, sent from Southend-on-Sea in September 1919, was designed by cartoonist Fred Spurgin and published by the Inter-Art Co.

194. Using a sporting situation to illustrate a phrase was a favourite trick of postcard artists in Edwardian days.

195. The word 'Football' was often used for Rugby in the first half of the 20th century, as on this cartoon by Fred Spurgin on a card from the Art & Humour Publishing Co. The pun in the caption would have been hugely appreciated by the contemporary audience.

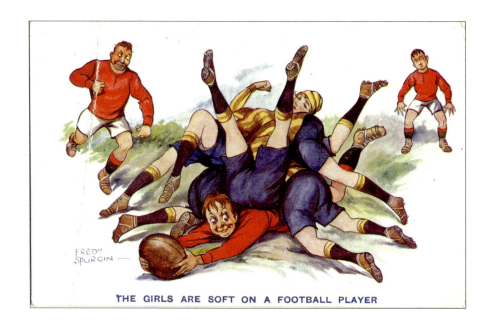

196. J.M. Staniforth featured a Welsh lady in costume on this Christmas greetings postcard from c.1908.

197. The first tour of England by a professional New Zealand Rugby League team was in 1907-08, when they were known as 'the All Golds' (a reference to the fact that they were being paid) or the 'professional All Blacks'. The tourists played against Northern Union clubs in England and Wales, and won their first 13 games. Then they arrived at Wigan and went down 12-8. This comic card published by W. Smith of Wigan was presumably produced before the match as otherwise the result would surely have been emblazoned on the card. It is headlined by the then well-known catch-phrase 'My word if I catch you bending', emphasised by the scrum situation included in the cartoon. The postcard is worn and tattered, with one corner torn off, but is probably pretty scarce now. Bizarrely, it made its way to North America, where it was posted in September 1908 at Camden, New Jersey. As a postscript, the 'All Golds' name was re-introduced as the suffix to a semi-professional team in Gloucestershire that played in the RL third tier from 2013-17.

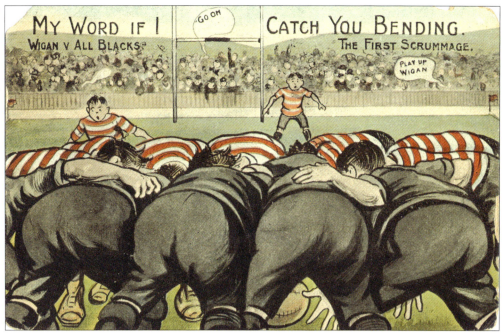

198. A French card, postally used in November 1903, illustrating 'Le Foot-Ball' and carrying heavy overtones of injury with patched-up players.

199. 'Sinjuns' was the phonetic name used for St. John's College at Cambridge University. An imaginative artist commemorated their rugby matches in the 1906-09 period with intricate designs, this one featuring imps, on which the score of the match (in this case 8-8) and the St. John's team was inscribed.

200. A postcard published in New Zealand in the 'Graphic series' commemorating the home side's 9-3 success in the August 1904 Test Match in Wellington.

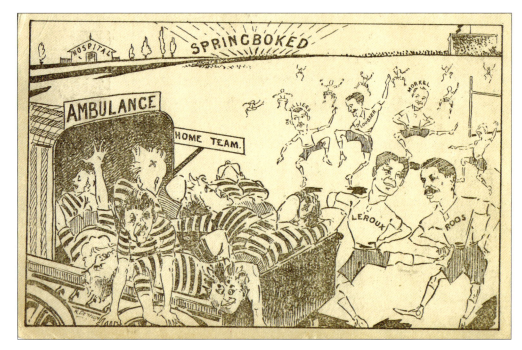

201. A rather unpleasant South African postcard predicting the likely outcome of the Springboks' first Rugby tour of the British Isles. The cartoonists' vision of the home side being carted off to hospital in an ambulance made the pre-tour talk of a series of 'friendly' matches redundant! The card was posted to Miss J. McLaren in Otago, New Zealand in November 1906.

202. Published in France, this card shows a spectator at a Rugby match telling us he wouldn't have quite so much trouble as the players in taking out a ball.

203 and 204. Left and below: two more postcards published by Millar & Lang. 'Scrimmage' was the term used for what we now call a scrum. No artist was credited on the cards issued by this Glasgow publisher.

205. From the same publisher, this card was posted from Notting Hill to Bayswater in January 1908.

206. More Rugby action from Millar & Lang - a situation that every player has been in! The card was posted at Northampton in October 1909.

207. Another postcard from the Glasgow publisher, prolific in their Rugby output. 'Take him low' is the phrase of the moment in the Union game, with surfacing issues about concussion problems and players suffering with dementia. The Rugby Football Union has issued a 'below the waist' edict for season 2023-4 for all matches below the Championship. They would surely have approved of this postcard.

208. Published by W.P. Spalding of Cambridge, this cartoon was obviously aimed at a University ethos of what constituted work!

Modern postcards

Collectors tend to divide picture postcards into two categories - old and modern, though the time zones are quite elastic. The older cards (let's say pre-1950) are generally much more expensive and have a smaller size (140 x 90mm compared with 150 x 100 for a more modern example). They tend to be monochrome and are more likely to have been postally used, which always makes the item more attractive. Modern cards will likely be in full colour and much more easily available, though there are many exceptions - for example, the only postcards I've come across that commemorated the first Rugby Union World Cup, some cartoons from France, were published in limited edition and hard to find now. Rugby collectors are fortunate that so many postcards have appeared over the past 70 years (especially the past 40), at a time when fewer and fewer cards are actually sent through the post. Most postcards since 1980 have featured the Rugby Union version. These modern examples can normally be picked up for a modest 50p-£2 each, though a few will rate more.

209. Postcards showing women playing Rugby are apparently almost non-existent. How is it that hardly any seem to be available of current international or club teams? The card on the left, one of very few I've ever seen, features Headingley Women's Rugby Union team, formed in 1988. It was published by The Women's Sports Foundation.

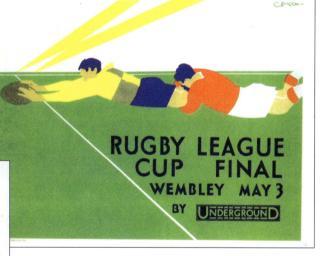

210. Modern yet vintage. This postcard, published by the London Transport Museum c. 1990, reproduces a poster advertising transport to the 1930 Rugby League Cup Final.

211. From Germany comes this postcard of the Championship Final (not dated) with an image of the St. Pauli club women in action against SC Neuenheim.

212. Right: Kings Cross Steelers, the world's first gay Rugby Club, pictured in 1998. The reverse of the card has the fixture list for the season, so it's not strictly speaking a postcard that could be sent through the post.

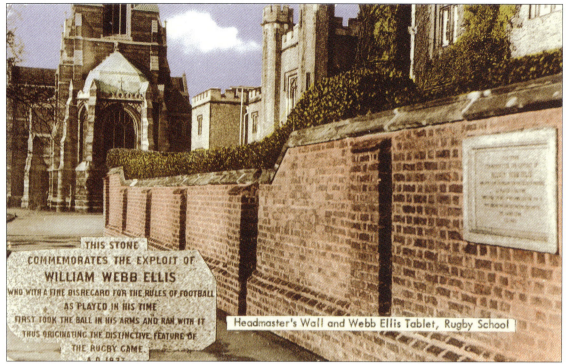

213. William Webb Ellis started it, so the story goes, when he caught a football and ran with it! The story dates from 1823 and may be a little apochryphal - it must have occurred to other boys, surely! This postcard published by the Midland View Co. of Market Harborough illustrates the stone on the Headmaster's Wall at Rugby School.

The Rugby Football Union celebrated its centenary in 1971, and Royal Mail issued a special commemorative stamp, used here on a first day cover envelope with special Twickenham postmark of 25th August that year.

214. Postcard publisher F. Loubatieres of Toulouse published this card as part of a 'Life in Toulouse' series. It shows on the right the celebrated French international Jean-Pierre Rives. The card, published in a limited edition of 1,500, was posted to Paris in December 1985.

215. Action from the match between France and the All Blacks at Tarbes in 1973. Another postcard from the same Toulouse publisher.

216. Right: Rugby Union in Aquitaine on a card from Editions Rex of Pau.

217. Left: William 'Dusty' Hare was a famous Rugby Union player for Newark, Leicester and England. Card published by J/V Postcards.

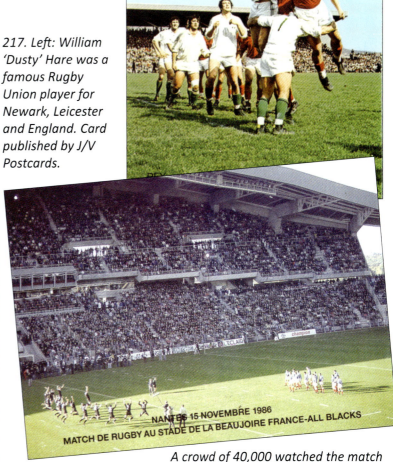

A crowd of 40,000 watched the match between France and the All Blacks At Nantes in 1986. France won 16-3. The picture shows the All Blacks team performing the Haka.

218. The world-famous Haka performed in the air, with words in the caption below. An official postcard from the New Zealand Rugby Union.

219. A postcard from Il Grande Rugby (a DVD series) in association with La Gazzetta dello Sport, published c.2000.

220. A pre-stamped New Zealand Post issue, featuring the Auckland Blues, one of the Super 12 franchises.

221. Australian Rugby postcard published in 2001 showing action from the Wallabies-Lions Test at Stadium Australia in Sydney.

222. Stuart Barnes scores the winning try for Bath in the 1989 Pilkington Cup Final. Bath beat Leicester 10-6. Card published by Enterprise Postcards.

223. Postcards of rugby teams are rarely issued by the clubs themselves now - profits on shirt merchandising are more efficient - but this is an interesting example from the late 1990s featuring Castleford Tigers. One of their most famous players, Danny Orr, is shown left.

224. Rugby League transformed itself into 'Super League' in 1996 after a couple of years of acrimonious wrangling over the future of the game and a massive injection of cash from Sky TV. This is the St. Helens team of 1996, winners of the first Super League. Saints have won the sport's Grand Final ten times and been losing finalists five times in the 27 years of the competition. Postcard published by Sports Maestros.

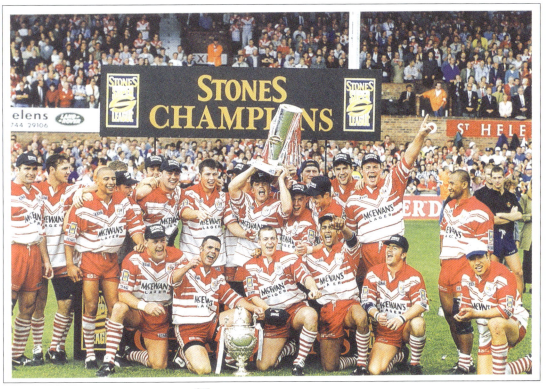

225. Cardiff Arms Park on a c.1990 postcard published by Judges of Hastings. Until the Millennium Stadium was built, this ground hosted scores of memorable internationals.

226. Aerial view of Scotland's national stadium, Murrayfield, on a card published by Skysnaps Aerial Photography. Murrayfield hosted matches at the 1991 World Cup, including the semi-final, when England beat the hosts 9-6.

227. Stradey Park, Llanelli, from above. This was an iconic Welsh stadium, the home of Llanelli RFC and later the Scarlets regional team. In 2008, though, a new stadium, Parc yr Scarlets, was built and Stradey Park demolished in 2010. The space is now a housing estate. This postcard was published by the Llanelli club (normally spelt 'Llanelly' on older postcards).

228. Pontypool RFC ground on a postcard from isle of Wight firm J. Arthur Dixon, posted to Trowbridge in June 1988. Though the club is now a feeder for the Dragons regional team, it has a long and famous history, having produced lots of Welsh international players. Probably its most famous trio of players was the famed front row of the 1970s - Bobby Windsor, Graham Price and Charlie Faulkner.

229. Newlands Rugby Stadium, Cape Town, South Africa, which hosted many internationals. Rugby is no longer played there - in fact, it seems almost certain that the complex will soon be demolished and the site redeveloped.

230. In the late 20th century, Amsterdam firm Art Unlimited published thousands of artworks as postcards. This is Pyke Koch's 'Scrum IV'. The original is in the Central Museum, Utrecht.

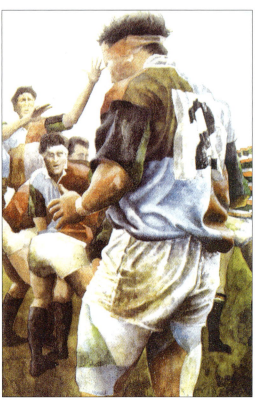

231. Rugby has always inspired artists. This study of Brian Moore (Nottingham, Harlequins and England) at a line-out was painted by Gareth Ball and published as a postcard in 1994 for the Picture Postcard Centenary Exhibition in London.

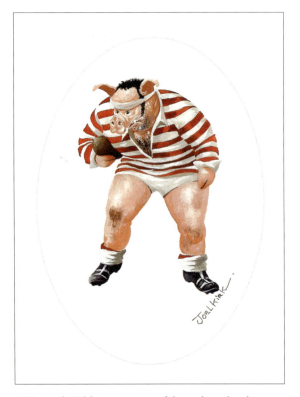

232. Joel Kirk's piggy prop (though today he might pop up as a wing or centre!) on a postcard published by Quay Publications of Poole, Dorset.

233. Modern French postcards are often published in very limited quantities aimed at the collector market. This study by artist Bernard Lejolly was limited to 150 postcards, published by Edition des Escargophiles. The scrum-half study features Welsh legend Gareth Edwards.

234. Italy were added to the European Five Nations Championship in the year 2000, and this postcard was published by the Italian Olympic Philatelic Society to celebrate the landmark.

235. A study of Philippe Sella by celebrated French artist 'Devo' in a series 'Le Sport en Fete'. Card published by '36 Bis' of Grisolles, France.

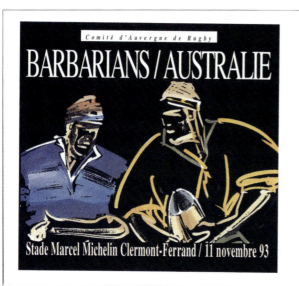

236. Lots of postcards were published in France as souvenirs of specific matches. This one came from the Comité d'Auvergne de Rugby in a limited 1,000 edition for the Barbarians-Australia match at Clermont-Ferrand in November 1993.

237. A postcard representing French Rugby League side St. Esteve.

238. Published by Cart'Com, a French firm that issued promotional freecards, this image by artist Nadine Rusé previews the 2004 Six Nations contest between France and Italy in Paris.

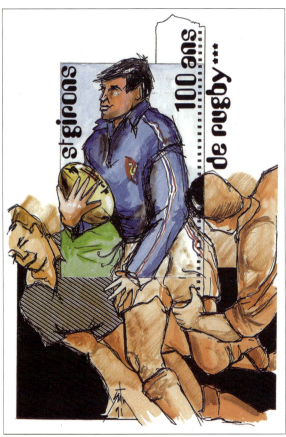

239. One hundred years of Rugby at St. Girons was celebrated on this postcard by artist Etienne Quentin, published by Group 7 of St. Denis.

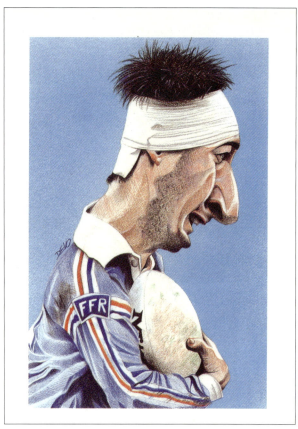

240. French international Philippe St. André on another postcard from Devo in the 'Le Sport en Fete' series.

241. Twickenham's Museum of Rugby launched its own series of postcards in the early 2000's, featuring cartoon characters in the 'Twickenham Pack' series. Romeo was flagged up as a winger, while other characters were Arthur, Lofty, Earl, Tricks and Brick - who invented those names?

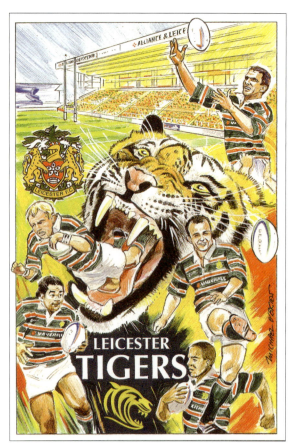

242. Michael O'Brien was a graphic illustrator until he turned his hand to picture postcards. This design, published by Reflections of a Bygone Age, celebrated the all-conquering Leicester Tigers team of the late 1990s.

243. A five-card set published by Maximum Original Co. celebrated Rugby League Clubs. This one, designed by artist Stuart Smith, focuses on Wakefield Trinity and shows a profile of their long-time home (since 1895) Belle Vue. Players illustrated are Jonty Parkin (top left), Billy Batten (bottom left) and Neil Fox.

244. Peter Morgan painted a series of player caricatures for postcards that were published by Rugly's of Swansea at the time of the 1999 World Cup. One set of seven featured Welsh players, another English, while a separate set of 20 included one player from each of the teams competing in the World Cup that year. Of the three players shown here, Allan Bateman and Scott Gibbs had both turned professional to play Rugby League with Warrington and St. Helens respectively before returning to Union for the 1999 event.

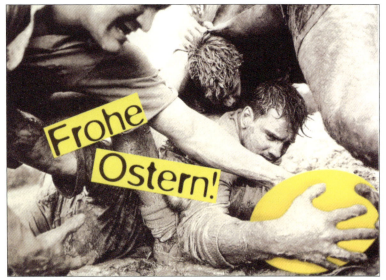

245. A Happy Easter postcard published by Deutsche Post. Compare this 'rugby ball as egg' design with the Donald McGill cartoon on p.74.

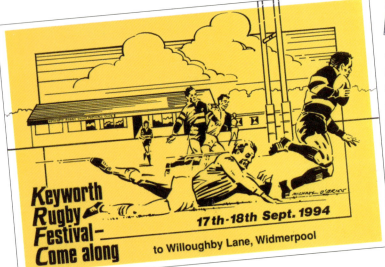

246. Italian postcard published to mark the 35th anniversary of a youth Rugby tournament at Rovigo, 50 miles south-west of Venice. The back has a special postal cancellation to commemorate the event, along with a Rugby-themed stamp.

247. Michael O'Brien design for a postcard promoting a weekend Rugby Union Festival at the Keyworth, Nottinghamshire, club, in September 1994.

248. Rob Andrew's drop goal against Australia in the 1995 World Cup was the subject of Rosi Robinson's batik on cotton design on this postcard.

World Cup postcards

This event came late to Rugby Union, with the first World Cup not held until 1987, over three decades later than the Rugby League version. Held in Australia and New Zealand, the first RU version was won, predictably, by New Zealand, who beat France in the Final. NZ have now won the competition three times, as have South Africa, while Australia have gained two successes and England one. The event has struggled sometimes to provide competitive games, with only half-a-dozen nations normally having a realistic chance of making the semi-finals.

Rugby League's first World Cup was held in France in 1954, the hosts losing to Great Britain 12-16 at Parc des Princes, Paris. In the 16 competitions so far held, Australia have won 12, Britain three and New Zealand one - an even more restricted list of champions. The sport has, however, been more innovative, and for its most recent tournament added wheelchair Rugby (a massive spectator success) to the existing mens' and womens' events.

The RU Womens' World Cup is maturing, but also struggling to have enough competitive sides.

Postcards of RU World Cups have been quite plentiful during the past 36 years, but the RL version hardly appears in the medium.

249. One of a set of six postcards published by Edition Combes of Sarlat, France, to mark the first Rugby Union World Cup, held in Australia and New Zealand in May/June 1987. Design was by Alain Carrier. The cards were published in a very limited edition, and are scarce now.

250. Another 1987 postcard, designed by Jean Luc Perrigault and published by Edition des Escargophiles.

251. In 1999 Australia won the World Cup, beating France 35-12 at the newly-opened Millennium Stadium, Cardiff. This postcard, published by Maurice Tanner and designed by Stuart Smith, shows Her Majesty Queen Elizabeth II presenting the Cup to John Eales.

252. The very first Rugby Union World Cup was held in Australia and New Zealand in 1987, though 33 years earlier a Rugby League version was inaugurated in France.
New Zealand and France reached the 1987 Final, the former winning 29-9.

253. Another postcard from the set of six published by Editions Combes of Sarlat, with Alain Carrier again the artist. Only 300 copies were printed, so this is likely to be a very rare example.

254. In the late 20th century, Royal Mail offered a free postcard printing service, where anyone could have a favourite photo produced as a card. The offer was limited to 20 copies per picture, though, so these are not plentiful! Pete Davies, already a postcard publisher and dealer, had a number of photos from the 1991 Rugby Union World Cup produced in this way. This one shows action from the New Zealand v. Scotland match at Cardiff Arms Park.

255. The 1995 event in South Africa was very well-covered on picture postcards. South Africa Post published postcards of each competing team in the 1995 World Cup. This is the Japan offering, with the Scottish postcard below right.
    Procard published postcards showing action scenes, Ruggles the mascot, players and grounds.

256. Michael O'Brien's design for the 1991 World Cup, featuring players from the four semi-finalists. In the Final at Twickenham (which I was fortunate enough to attend!), Australia beat England 12-6.

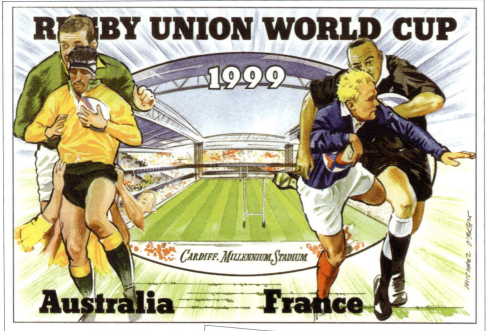

258. The 1999 Rugby Union World Cup was the most post-carded, largely thanks to publishers Rugly's and Reflections of a Bygone Age. The latter issued 21 cards, one for each competing country and another, shown here, for the Final, while Rugly's produced 34. This card features the four semi-finalists. Australia beat France 35-12 in the Final, while South Africa won the third-place play-off, beating New Zealand 22-18.

259. One of the single-country cards designed by Michael O'Brien, this one featuring Wales and Rob Howley (though this example has been signed by flanker Martyn Williams). Each of the 20 cards in the main series comprised one of the stadia in the British Isles and France used for the tournament, a country's shirt and crest, and a player or players.

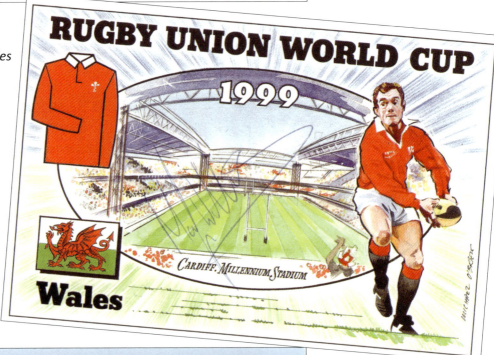

260. Royal Mail Stamp Card series D15, published in October 1999. The artist was Peter Sutton. The reverse has a souvenir cancellation from the Stamp Show at Earl's Court, London, the following May, and has been posted with, appropriately, a 1st class stamp showing the Welsh Dragon.

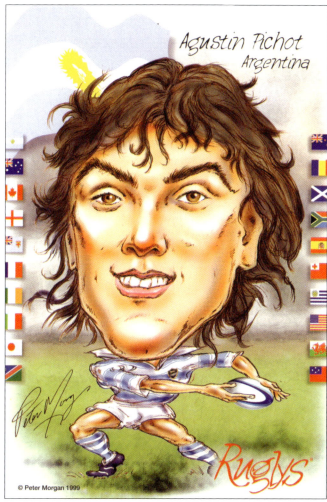

261. One of Rugly's individual cards for the 1999 tournament, representing Argentina with Peter Morgan's caricature of scrum-half Agustin Pichot.

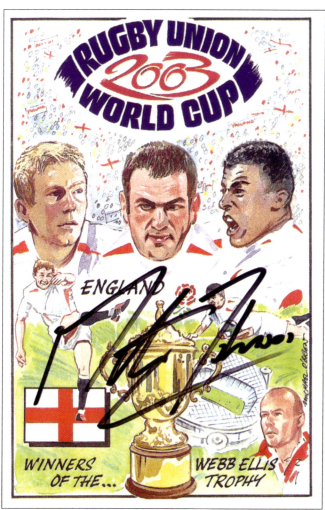

262. A montage painting by Michael O'Brien, one of six postcards published by Reflections of a Bygone Age for the 2003 World Cup. The design profiles Jonny Wilkinson (with the famous match-winning drop goal), Martin Johnson, the England captain (who has signed this example) and Jason Robinson, who scored England's try in the Final, where Australia were beaten 20-17. Coach Clive Woodward also appears on the card.

263. The same three players also appeared on Stuart Smith's design published by Maurice Tanner, one of a series of eight. The card also includes the set of Royal Mail stamps issued to mark the occasion.

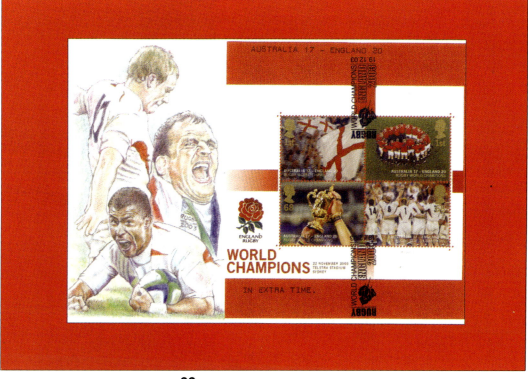

264. ColR Cards specialised in limited-run commemoratives and published this one for the England-South Africa Final in the 2007 RUWC. South Africa won 15-6.

265. There have been very few postcards commemorating any of Rugby League's World Cups, though Maximum Original Co. published this example for the 1995 RLWC in October 1995, the design by Stuart Smith.

266. A major monthly postcard collectors' fair has been held at a series of hotels near Russell Square in London for many years, and until 2013 the then organisers, IPM Promotions, issued a souvenir card for each fair, often featuring contemporary events. The October 2011 postcard portrayed a scene from the RUWC Final that month, played at Eden Park, Auckland, on the day of that month's fair. New Zealand beat France 8-7.

267. A rarity! A postcard of the New Zealand Black Ferns women's Rugby team for the 2002 World Cup held in Barcelona. This was the second women's event and the Black Ferns duly retained their title as 16 nations competed for the prize.

Modern postcards with an advert focus

Picture postcards using Rugby as an advertising link provide a rich source of images for a collector, with major brands and names sponsoring big events. The following four pages provide just a sample of these. Most were originally available free of charge, being given away as promotional items, but when available now may cost a pound or more each. eBay is one source for many of these.

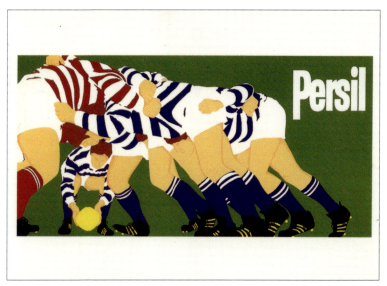

269. Persil manufacturers Lever Bros. used Rugby as a promotion for their washing powder brand. Postcard published by Drumahoe Graphics.

268. Boomerang Media have published over many years tens of thousands of postcards promoting products and given away free in racks in bars, restaurants, cinemas, and health and leisure clubs. In 2003, the firm issued 15 distinctively-designed cards for Adidas using players from the RUWC that year. This is no. 11, Jonah Lomu.

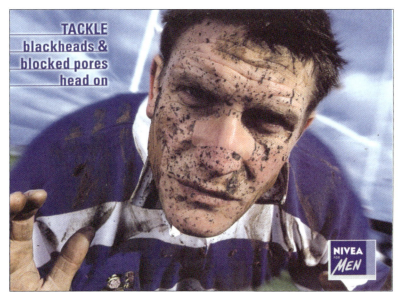

270. This postcard came with a sample sachet of Nivea clear pore strips on the back!

271. Martin Johnson was no. 4 in the Boomerang series.

272. Many posters were commissioned by London Transport to advertise events in the capital and promote The Underground. This postcard, published by The London Transport Museum (LTM 502) reproduces a 1929 poster designed by D. Paton for the Rugby League Cup Final at Wembley that year, the first to be held there. Wigan beat Dewsbury 13-2. A programme for the game sold at Sotheby's in 2009 for £180. This postcard for the RL final features a line-out, though. It looks like the artist got her wires crossed!

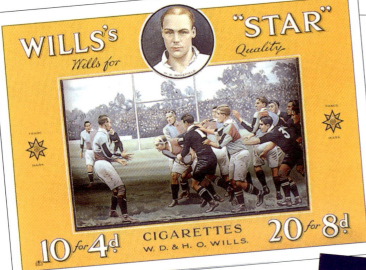

273. Once upon a time cigarettes were promoted as providing a healthy lifestyle, as on this Wills poster, published as a postcard by the Robert Opie Collection. England international Wavell Wakefield is pictured on the design, and Harlequins are one of the teams in the match situation.

274. Postcard advert issued by Tennent's Breweries for the Scottish Cup Final (year unclear). International player Rob Wainwright is on the picture side, and invites rugby fans to attend in a facsimile note on the reverse.

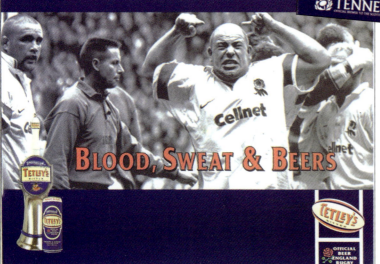

275. This looks suspiciously like Richard Cockerill, long-term Leicester player and coach until he was sacked in 2016, went to Toulon as coach, and then, in 2017, Edinburgh as head coach. This Tetley's advertising postcard was posted at Derby in November 2006.

276. Schweppes tonic water advert published on a postcard in France by Ubique Group. The photo of an Ireland-Wales match at Dublin was taken by Peter Windfield.

277. Brains Brewery's wishful thinking, marketed as 'positive thinking'. The only downside was that England actually won the Six Nations match on 22nd February 2003 by 26 points to 9!

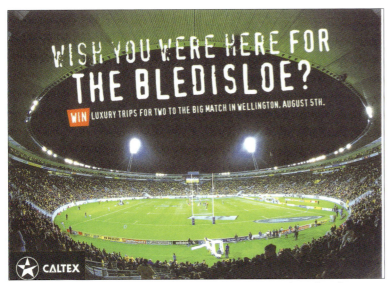

278. Postcard advertising a competition to win tickets for the New Zealand-Australia Bledisloe Cup match at Wellington in the year 2000.

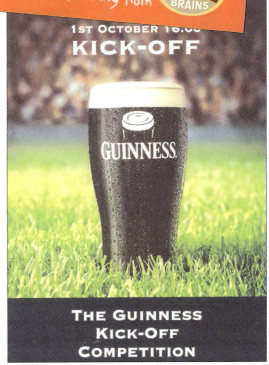

279. Guinness were one of the official sponsors of the 1999 RUWC. This postcard was issued to promote the brand in South Africa.

280. A French sandwich bar chain promoted beach rugby on this 2014 postcard.

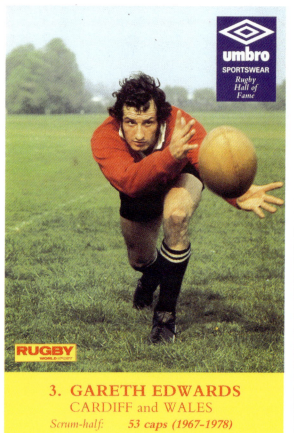

281. Foster's Beer was the 'official' drink for the 1998 Hong Kong Sevens, and this associated postcard published by Cardrac, a freecard issuer, promotes the brand. No artist is credited with the cartoon.

282 and 283. Right and above right: two postcards from a Rugby World Magazine series sponsored by Umbro Sportswear in the 1970s, featuring the sports manufacturer's 'Hall of Fame'. Gareth Edwards and Mervyn Davies are featured here.

104

A comic miscellany

Rugby has continued to provide inspiration for comic postcards up to the present day, as the selection on the following four pages shows. Offering a wider variety of designs than the Edwardian output, these postcards are also much easier to find. A large number originate from France, where there is still a rich tradition of artists specialising in this medium.

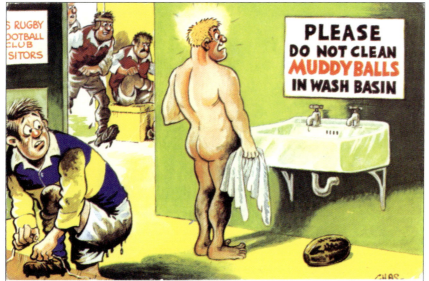

284 and 285. Playwright John Godber's 'Up and Under' was based on a Rugby League pub seven-a-side team. It was first staged in Hull in 1984, but this postcard (above) advertises a production by the Harrogate Theatre Company in 1992. (left): advert for the movie version at Odeon cinemas, published by Boomerang Media, which specialised in the distribution of free advertising postcards in the late 20th century.

286. A classic postcard cartoon with innuendo by Charles Grigg ('Chas') published by Bamforth in their 'Comic' series. This card was posted at Bournemouth in 1992.

287. A fantasy Rugby team from a French publisher.

288. Bamforth 'Comic' series postcard drawn by Arnold Taylor, who was the Holmfirth company's staff artist for many years.

289. A neat play on the word 'conversion' - French double-entendre. Postcard published c.1957 by a French company called Photochrom.

290. One of the 'Anatomy' series postcards published by John Hinde and designed by Arthur Pickering.

291. League or Union? Let's say League, because the comic design was by Leeds artist Fred Camp and published in that city by JT Postcards. Card no. 1 in 'Wild Flowers' series.

292. No. 62 in a 'Classic Cornwall' series that displayed stage-managed photos by Ashley Peters. Most featured Cornish pasties in some way.

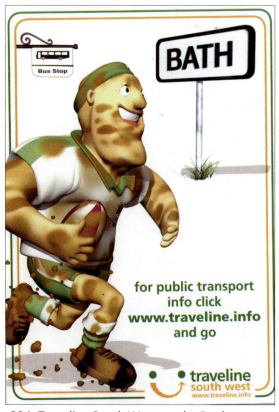

293. Jean Claval is a prolific French postcard artist. This card, published by Edition des Escargophiles, is titled 'Vive le rugby'.

294. Traveline South West used a Rugby connection, specifically Bath RFC, to promote their public transport services.

295. Wouldn't it be nice? The kicker receives a bit of assistance on this comic postcard from Rainbow Cards.

WELCOME TO TWICKENHAM

298. 'Scrum-time' on this design published by Rainbow Cards.

296. 'Rugby Tales' is one of the shiny 'Dufex' series postcards published by F.J. Warren of Hitchin. The Welsh Dragon in all its glory!

297. Rupert Besley is an Isle of Wight illustrator who designed hundreds of comic seaside and holiday postcards for publishers J. Arthur Dixon. This Rugby-themed cartoon was adapted for at least three different countries, England, Scotland and Wales.

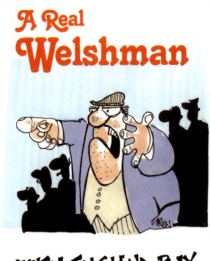

299. The 'A Real Welshman' series was fun while it lasted. The cards were published by Funfare Press of Cardiff. The artist is 'Gren' (Grenville Jones of the 'South Wales Echo'), whose annual Rugby calendars were legendary.

'WELCOME TO SCOTLAND!'

301. Besley's Rugby Scotland version of the fierce front row.

300. This postcard was published in Wales (by Pembrokeshire Eye of Haverfordwest). It turns the scoreboard on its head as it flags up pints of blood lost. Hence England's superior score! The artist is uncredited. Card posted at Carmarthen in April 1994.

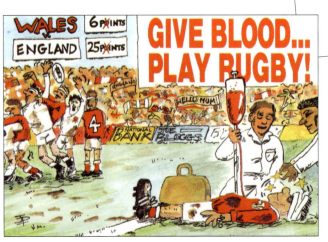

An extra time miscellany

302. Another Rosi Robinson postcard based on a Batik on cotton print.

303. On the back of this postcard, Sevenoaks School claim to have 'pioneered the first British Rugby tour to Australia (1976) and Round the world' (1980). Maybe they should clarify that claim a bit? This postcard was posted at Tonbridge in December 1992.

304. Barefoot Rugby at Grey Junior School in South Africa, with under-13s in action. This card was posted in April 1993.

305. 'Rugby Final', a photo by Paul France, published by Black & White Images Ltd of London W3.

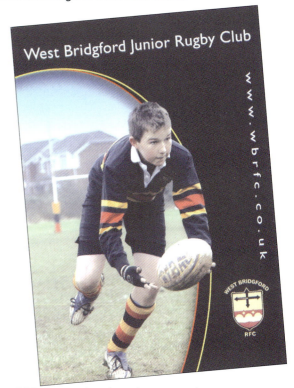

306. Promotional card encouraging youngsters to join West Bridgford (Nottingham) club junior section.

307. (right): the 2005 Rugby League Challenge Cup Final, held at Cardiff's Millennium Stadium because Wembley was being rebuilt, featured Leeds, the overwhelming favourites, and Hull, coached by John Kear, who won 25-24. Kear already had form in big games, having previously coached Sheffield Eagles to an improbable Cup Final win over Wigan in 1998.

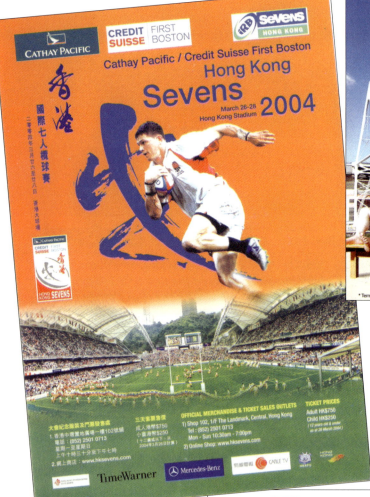

308. (left): Promotional postcard for the 2004 Hong Kong RU Sevens Tournament. The location was crucial in promoting the worldwide popularity of Sevens.

309. Hong Kong became a mecca for high profile tournaments in the shortened version of the game in the early 21st century. This one, published by gocart hk, flagged up a Ten's tournament in 2007.

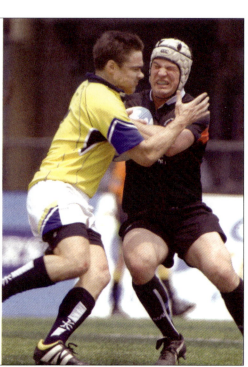

310. In 1997 model Linda Evangelista teamed up with toiletries company Yardley, official suppliers of aftershave and toiletries to the British Lions team that toured South Africa in 1997.

311. Mick Wright of Leicester designed 16 caricatures of Leicester Tigers players in 1999 and published them himself as picture postcards. This one features Austin Healey, though I'm not sure I would have recognised him. Healey works as a pundit on TV covering Premiership matches now.

312. Published by Boomerang Media, this postcard is actually an advert promotion for Leeds Metropolitan University (students rubbing shoulders with champions). Their 'low charging, high impact' pitch was illustrated by this Leeds Rhinos RL duo Barrie McDermott (with ball) and Danny Maguire, two stars in a highly successful team that also included Kevin Sinfield (now England RU defence coach) and mercurial scrum-half Rob Burrow. This pair's friendship and fund-raising efforts for MND research have been amazing.

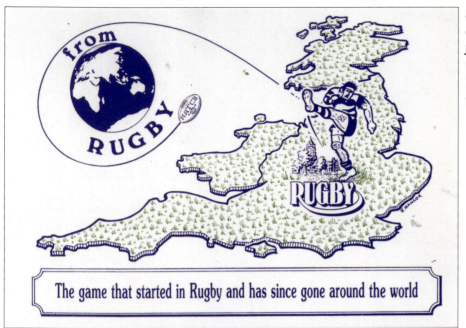

313. An appropriate end to our tour around 120 years of picture postcards featuring the game of Rugby. This card was published by Rugby & District Tourist Association to encourage visitors to the town.

314 and 315. Closing time - a couple of postcards published by John French showing pub signs at (left) Castleford and (right) Swinton in Rugby League territory.

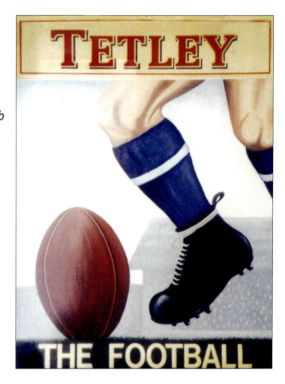

I hope you've enjoyed this book, presenting a different focus on the game of Rugby. Reflections of a Bygone Age publish a range of books based on picture postcards, featuring Sport, Transport and villages, towns and cities in England. For a full listing, visit our website www.postcardcollecting.co.uk
where you will also find details of Rugby postcards we publish.

Brian Lund
May 2023